Natives & Newcomers

The Way We Lived in North Carolina before 1770

*Library of Congress Cataloging in
Publication Data*

Fenn, Elizabeth A. (Elizabeth Anne),
1959–
  Natives & newcomers.

  Bibliography: p.
  1. North Carolina—History—Colo-
nial period, ca. 1600–1775. 2. North
Carolina—Social life and customs.
3. North Carolina—Description and
travel—1891–   —Guide-books.
4. Historic sites—North Carolina—
Guide-books. I. Wood, Peter H.,
1943– . II. Nathans, Sydney.
III. North Carolina. Dept. of Cultural
Resources. IV. Title. V. Title
Natives and newcomers.
F257.F46 1983   975.6′02   82-20128
ISBN 0-8078-1549-7
ISBN 0-8078-4101-3 (pbk.)

Natives & Newcomers

The Way We Lived in North Carolina before 1770

Published for the North Carolina Department of Cultural Resources

by The University of North Carolina Press   *Chapel Hill*

Editor:
Sydney Nathans

Consultants:
Larry Misenheimer
William S. Price, Jr.

This publication has been made possible through a grant from the National Endowment for the Humanities.

The Way We Lived series was developed under the guidance of the Historic Sites Section, Division of Archives and History, North Carolina Department of Cultural Resources.

(Title page) Delft plate, ca. 1760, Owens House, Halifax, Halifax County.

(Right) Colonial fan made of hand-painted paper and mother of pearl. N.C. State Archives.

Christine Alexander took the photographs not otherwise credited in this book.

Text by Elizabeth A. Fenn and Peter H. Wood

Research and Marginalia by Jean B. Anderson

Design and Art Editing by Christine Alexander

Wash day. Benjamin Butterworth, *The Growth of Industrial Arts* (Washington, D.C., 1892).

Experiencing History

This series of books, *The Way We Lived*, is based on the premise that the past can be most fully comprehended through the combined impact of two experiences: reading history and visiting historic places. The text of this volume (the first in a series of five) is therefore coordinated with a variety of historical sites. Most places pictured as well as those mentioned in the margins are open to the public regularly or by appointment. Information about visiting and exact locations may be obtained locally.

Our objective in specifying sites has not been to compile a complete or comprehensive catalogue of historic places in the state; rather it has been to guide the reader to a representative selection of sites that exemplify the major themes of the text.

Many excellent examples that might have served our purpose equally well have been omitted. Others now in the planning or working stages of restoration may be expected to swell the number of unnamed sites. We can only leave to the readers the pleasure of their discovery and the hope that this volume will serve as a stimulus to further reading and exploration.

Contents

The Outer Banks.

Cape Hatteras National Seashore comprises twenty-eight thousand acres on the famed Outer Banks, including Bodie, Hatteras, and Ocracoke islands.

The First Carolinians

For almost five hundred years, people of European and African descent have inhabited a land now called North Carolina. Richly varied, it extends from the eastern edges of the Mississippi River basin in the Appalachian Mountains to the remarkable barrier islands known as the Outer Banks. Mount Mitchell, near the Blue Ridge Parkway in Pisgah National Forest, is the highest elevation in the eastern United States. Here northern hardwoods mingle on the steep slopes with a bewildering variety of southern flowers and shrubs. Less than five hundred miles east, at Cape Hatteras, a venerable lighthouse surveys the flat but treacherous coastline. Here the warm waters of the powerful Gulf Stream bring mild, and occasionally stormy, weather to the low-lying coast. Between the rugged Blue Ridge and the broad Coastal Plain, stretching roughly from modern-day Morganton to Raleigh, lie the rolling foothills that colonial settlers called the Carolina Piedmont.

Thousands of years before settlers from Europe and Africa set foot on Carolina soil, another people inhabited the land. Mistakenly termed "Indians" by Christopher Columbus, they were in fact the first Carolinians. Their history encompasses migrations the length and breadth of an immense continent, shattering invasions, and technological transformation. By the time non-Indians reached North Carolina, sound agricultural methods were well in place. Even metalworking was not unknown.

Perhaps the best way to begin the study of North Carolina Indian history is by listening to the Indians themselves. North American Indians had no written languages. They could not store their history in dusty volumes on the shelves of ancient libraries. Instead, they recorded their history orally, in the stories and legends they passed from generation to generation. It is this tradition which kept the Indian past alive.

One such story comes from the Tuscarora Indians, who lived in the vicinity of the Neuse River. The legend records a long, icy migration from a land far to the west. It was told to a modern Tuscarora man by his great-grandmother.

In the old world, the legend says, there was a long famine. Nothing would grow, and people were starving. Finally the people held a council meeting. The council decided that the people had to leave their homeland for a new place, where they could find food.

After walking some distance, the people realized they were walking on ice. For days they walked on ice. One group got tired and

"This Part of Carolina is faced with a Chain of Sand-Banks, which defends it from the Violence and Insults of the Atlantic Ocean; by which Barrier a vast Sound is hemmed in, which fronts the Mouths of the Navigable and Pleasant Rivers of this Fertile Country, and into which they disgorge themselves. . . . Some of their Channels admit only of Sloops, Brigantines, and Small Barks and Ketches; and such are Currituck, Ronoak, and up the Sound above Hatteras; Whilst others can receive Ships of Burden, as Ocacock, Topsail-Inlet, and Cape-Fair, as appears by my Chart." Lawson, *A New Voyage to Carolina.*

Mount Mitchell, Mount Mitchell State Park, Yancey County, is the highest peak in the eastern United States, reaching 6,684 feet. It is named for Professor Elisha Mitchell (1793–1857), of the University of North Carolina, who explored the Carolina mountains and estimated the height of many peaks, including Mount Mitchell.

decided not to go on. The other group decided to keep walking—to "where the sun rises"—until they found food. They walked during the day and at night they rested.

At last they stopped. Ahead of them was a black streak, which they thought might be a huge snake. For safety, they spread apart within hearing distance of one another. When the front persons reached the streak, they learned it was not a snake, but a lush forest with abundant food. The message was relayed to the end of the line, and the group gathered at the forest. They found so much food that they decided to send for the others. But, when they returned to the west, they discovered that the ice had melted. At the place they had crossed, they saw only water. They had no way to reach their friends.

Another North Carolina tribe, the Cherokees, tell a similar story. Like the Tuscarora tale, it includes a long, eastward migration prompted by starvation. It even describes life in the north, wearing snowshoes and enduring the long darkness of subarctic winters.

Modern archeologists also think the ancestors of the North Carolina Indians may have migrated from the west. Although their theories vary considerably, most scholars agree on one fact: the predecessors of the American Indians at some time crossed a land bridge between Asia and America. Some say the first crossing, toward "where the sun rises," was more than 30,000 years ago. Indeed, it could have occurred as much as 70,000 years ago, when the growing glaciers of the last ice age lowered the sea level enough to expose dry land at the Bering Strait. At the peak of the ice age's final phase, about 18,000 years ago, the land bridge from Asia to present-day Alaska may have been 1,000 miles wide. It clearly would have been possible for inhabitants of Asia to reach North America.

From the Bering Strait, the first Americans probably migrated eastward several thousand miles, crossing the northernmost extension of what we now know as the Rocky Mountains. On the eastern side of the Rockies, they found a long, narrow corridor of ice-free land. Only fifty to a hundred miles wide in places, this corridor stretched far to the south alongside the mountains. The earliest Americans followed this route, finally emerging from the ice-covered north near present-day Montana.

The first North Carolinians arrived over ten thousand years ago. Unfortunately, little evidence of these people survives. The environment they encountered was very different from what we know today. Glacial ice still lay over much of North America. Although too far south to be ice-covered, the North Carolina region was nevertheless quite cold and wet. Even the animal population differed. Huge animals, such as the mastodon, roamed the land alongside more familiar game, such as deer.

These earliest North Carolinians are known as "Paleo-Indians."

Snow in the mountains.

They lived in bands of no more than fifty people, staying in one place while they could and moving to better food resources when necessary. With stone points bound to long wooden shafts, the Paleo-Indians hunted the large animals of the region. While Paleo-Indian hunters may have thrown their spears at animals from a distance, some scholars speculate that the hunters preferred to attack at extremely close range, where there was little chance of missing.

Not all large game hunting was done with spears. A favorite technique was to stampede a herd of animals over a cliff or other precipice, thus killing many at one time. Although these animals provided one source of food, a large part of the Paleo-Indian diet may have consisted of vegetables and small game.

The migrations of these ancient North Carolinians were not aimless. They followed herds of large animals, and returned to specific sites regularly. While some areas provided seasonal food resources, other locations, like Morrow Mountain in present-day Stanly County, supplied ideal stone for projectile points. At the top of Morrow Mountain, in Morrow Mountain State Park, visitors can still see the large rhyolite outcrops where North Carolina dwellers gathered

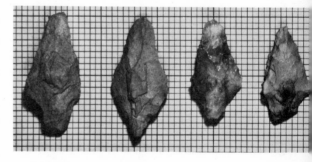

Morrow Mountain projectile points.
Archeology Branch, Division of Archives and History.

point material for over ten thousand years. Morrow Mountain and all the Uwharrie Mountains are unique for their numerous exposed deposits of rhyolite. At one time the Uwharries were volcanic mountains in a huge inland sea. The rhyolite outcrops were formed from fast-cooling lava.

As the ice age entered its last stages, North Carolina's climate warmed. By about 8000 B.C., the environment was much as it is today. In the meantime, North Carolinians had developed new ways of using the land's resources. A new tradition, called "Archaic" by archeologists, began to emerge. The people of the Archaic tradition may have been more sedentary than the Paleo-Indians. Because they relied increasingly on plant foods and small game, they did not have to follow the migrations of large animals so closely. They gathered seeds and nuts from the forest floor and developed fishing and trapping skills.

When they did hunt deer and other large animals, the Archaic people used a spear-throwing device called an "atlatl." By giving the hunter added leverage, the atlatl greatly increased the force with which the spear could be thrown. Weights of polished stone, shaped like butterflies or half-moons, were attached to the atlatl's shaft.

A great variety of projectile points and stone tools were made during the Archaic period. Many points now had basal stems, which could be more easily bound to a shaft. Stone flakes became sharp scraping tools. Flakes and discarded points, once rechipped, served as drills. Archaic artisans carved vessels out of soapstone and ground other stones for axe heads and atlatl weights. Even without fired clay

4

pots, they managed to boil water by placing hot rocks inside a stone or skin vessel.

Though these descendants of the first Carolinians appear to have adjusted admirably to life in southeastern North America, their culture was bound to change. New ideas and perhaps even contact with different people resulted in cultural developments. Although the changes were undoubtedly gradual, archeologists recognize the year 500 B.C. as the approximate end of the Archaic tradition. A new tradition, called "Woodland," had taken its place.

Because of the relative abundance of material remains, we know far more about the Woodland tradition than we do about its precursors. Unlike the people of the Archaic tradition, the Woodland people knew how to make pottery of clay collected from local river and stream beds. To make their clay more workable, these early potters used crushed clay grit as a tempering material. They learned to roughen the exterior of their pots with fabric-covered wooden paddles.

As ceramic techniques developed further, more vessels were made, and artisans began tempering their clay with sand. New materials adorned the paddles with which they finished their vessels. Even smoking pipes were formed from clay. Evidence suggests that prehistoric North Carolinians smoked tobacco in their clay pipes, and they may have smoked other plants as well.

Hunting efficiency increased dramatically in the Woodland tradition as the bow and arrow replaced the atlatl. Although hunting and gathering still filled a large part of the Woodland people's dietary needs, rudimentary forms of agriculture supplemented this fare. Native plants such as the sunflower were among the earliest domesticated crops. Tobacco also may have been grown with some regularity before the time of Christ.

By A.D. 1200 North Carolinians were wholeheartedly committed to an agricultural economy. However, the serious pursuit of agriculture meant a changed way of life. Cultivated corn, beans, and squash required almost constant care during the growing season. Consumption of meat declined, and seasonal wandering dwindled. North Carolinians began to settle in permanent dwellings. The dwellings, grouped in small villages along riverbanks, resembled what we today call "wigwams." A latticework of intertwined saplings covered by skins, bark, or other material formed the basic structure.

By excavating skeletal remains in ancient burial grounds, archeologists have determined that the people of the late Woodland period were the ancestors of tribes, such as the Catawba, who lived in North Carolina at the time of European contact. By this time, early in the sixteenth century, the Woodland tradition had yielded to the more modern traditions of the "Historic" period. Although they shared a common Woodland background and spoke related languages, each of

The experience of Carolina Indians was probably little different from that of the Mayas who lamented the old days before the white man's arrival: "There was then no sickness; they had no aching bones; they had then no high fever; they had then no smallpox; they had then no burning chest; they had then no abdominal pain; they had then no consumption; they had then no headache. At that time the course of humanity was orderly. The foreigners made it otherwise when they arrived here." Crosby, *The Columbian Exchange*.

Old engraving of tobacco. E. R. Billings, *Tobacco: Its History, Varieties, Culture* . . . (Hartford, 1875).

Town Creek Indian Mound and palisade, Town Creek State Historic Site, Montgomery County. N.C. State Archives.

An entrance to the Town Creek Indian Mound palisade.

the various groups across the North Carolina Piedmont had developed distinctive cultural traits. Scholars have found a great variety of linguistic traditions among North American Indians. While the Piedmont tribes spoke Siouan languages, other North Carolina tribes had Iroquoian and Algonquian linguistic heritages.

Even before the Siouan tribes of the Carolina Piedmont faced the main thrust of the European invasion, they had had to contend with another invading threat. From the region of present-day Alabama and Georgia came a group of Indians from a culture later called "Creek." Although the precise reason for their northward migration remains a mystery, it is possible that famine or other troubles had disrupted life in their home country. The Creek contingent reached North Carolina sometime near 1450. In the southern part of the state—present-day Richmond, Anson, and Montgomery counties—they uprooted local Siouan tribes and settled in the lush Pee Dee River Valley. In this rich agricultural basin, they built dwellings, planted crops, and raised children for a hundred years. Then, just as suddenly as they had arrived, they were gone. Even before the English attempted to settle at Roanoke, the Creek invaders had been driven from North Carolina. The Siouan tribes of the Piedmont had reclaimed their homeland.

At Town Creek Indian Mound near Mount Gilead, North Carolina, visitors can view reconstructed remains of the Pee Dee Creek culture. The Creeks chose this high bluff overlooking the Little River for the site of their regional ceremonial center. Basketload by basketload, they hauled earth from nearby fields and a swampy area to the west. Finally, they completed an earthen ceremonial lodge and surrounded it with a palisade of upright logs. After much use, the earthen lodge collapsed. Once again the people of the Pee Dee collected earth, this time to cover the lodge's remains. The mound they cre-

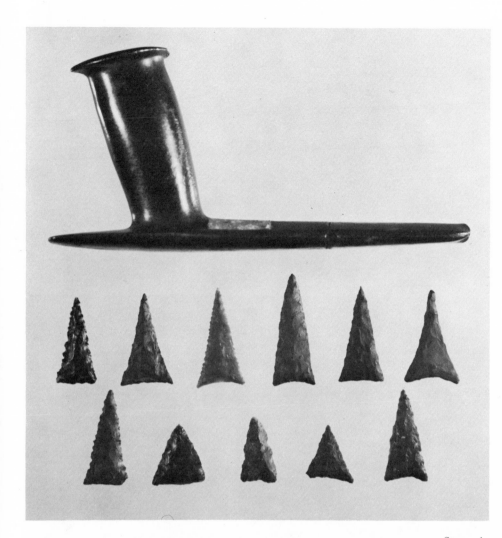

Stone pipe and small triangular projectile points of the Late Woodland Yadkin River site. Photograph by Linda Luster. Archeology Branch, Division of Archives and History.

ated in covering the lodge became the foundation for their next construction: a ceremonial temple. But this building, like the first, was ill-fated. When it burned to the ground, the Creeks covered the remains as they had previously and built a third temple atop the growing earth mound.

This third and final structure is the one visitors can see reconstructed at the site today. Priests kept a sacred fire smoldering in the temple year-round. Once a year, the Creek people held their vital green corn, or "busk," celebration at the Town Creek center. The celebration, which lasted about a week, was one of renewal and purification for the year to come. Held at the first harvest of corn, the busk celebration involved fasting, ceremonial baths, and imbibing the "Black Drink." All the village fires and the sacred temple fire, polluted by a year's sins, were extinguished. After four days, the priests kindled a new fire. A great feast was held. Runners carried embers from the new fire to villages up and down the Pee Dee, and the

The "black drink" was a decoction made from the toasted leaves of various shrubs of the holly family, particularly the *ilex vomitoria*, an emetic. It was drunk by all mature males at the end of the third day, a day of fasting, in the four-day busk ceremony.

7

Ear spools worn by the Indians of the Pee Dee culture. Archeology Branch, Division of Archives and History.

Burial hut, Town Creek Indian Mound State Historic Site.

Creeks reignited local fires. It was because of this ceremony that the Creeks called themselves "people of one fire."

The busk ceremony occurred only once a year. For the remainder of the year, the Town Creek Indians lived as settled farmers. Only the high priest lived within the ceremonial center's palisade. The rest of the people clustered their dwellings in small villages throughout the river valley. The women, directed by overseers, cultivated corn, tobacco, beans, squash, and pumpkins in communal fields. Children played nearby, and infants spent their earliest days bound to cradleboards, a practice that produced a unique flattening of the skull among Creek and other Indians. Men practiced crafts such as woodworking.

Throughout the time they lived along the Pee Dee, the Creek Indians fought the Siouan tribes they had displaced. Intervillage rival-

Little River and turtles sunning on a fallen tree near the Town Creek Indian Mound, Montgomery County.

In the eighteenth century, William Bartram watched an Indian ceremony before a lacrosse game: "The people being assembled and seated in order, and the musicians having taken their station, the ball opens, first with a long harangue or oration spoken by an aged chief in commendation of the manly exercise of the ball-play, recounting the many and brilliant victories which the town of Cowe had gained over the other towns in the nation, not forgetting or neglecting to recite his own exploits, together with those of other aged men now present, coadjutors in the performance of these athletic games in their youthful days." Cruickshank, ed., *John and William Bartram's America.*

ries and feuds, however, were settled through another sort of contest. Called "the little brother of war," Indian stickball, or lacrosse, took on a seriousness we only rarely associate with sports today. Players often suffered traumatic injuries. Broken limbs were not uncommon. Beside the temple at Town Creek, still within the palisade, the ancient playing field used for lacrosse and other games is visible. A tall goalpost topped by a bear skull stands in front of the temple.

By 1550 the Town Creek people were gone. The Siouan tribes of the Piedmont had returned to their homelands of old. To the east, where the powerful Powhatan confederacy of Virginia would soon be pushing its way south, European sailors had made contact with local Algonquian Indians. To the west, Hernando de Soto, the Spanish explorer, had journeyed through the North Carolina mountains and contacted the Iroquoian-speaking Cherokee Indians. Before long the Tuscaroras, an Iroquoian tribe from the Neuse River region, would be carrying European trade goods to the Indians of the Piedmont where Town Creek once stood.

Lost Continent to Lost Colony

The first European explorers of North Carolina, like all early voyagers to the New World, did not find what they were actively seeking. Initially, they envisioned the discovery of an ocean pathway to the treasures of the East. It took Europeans almost a century to adjust their maps and their minds to the reality that they encountered on the Carolina coast: the sweet-scented edge of a massive continent.

In the autumn of 1492, while the men and women at Town Creek were occupied with the hard work and important rituals of the harvest season, Christopher Columbus and his crew sighted land in the Atlantic. Miscalculating, Columbus assumed that he had found the spice islands of Asia—known as the Indies. Three more voyages did not change his opinion, and he died believing that he had opened a new route to the Orient.

Those following in his wake labored to test and revise Columbus's vision. The Spaniards continued to call the local inhabitants "Indians." They extracted gold from them and demanded information of a passage farther westward to China. But they could find no western strait, only the landlocked Gulf of Mexico. Were Europeans separated from the Orient by inhabited continents they had never imagined? If so, could those lands offer up riches comparable to those of the East? Within thirty years, Spanish explorers provided all of Europe with answers to both questions. Hernando Cortez found and conquered the enormously rich Aztec Empire of central Mexico. In 1522 the ship of Ferdinand Magellan, having skirted the vast coastline of South America and crossed the Pacific, returned to Spain from its journey round the world.

The desire of rival states to emulate the Spanish discoveries brought the first Europeans to the Carolinas. The French hired their own skilled Italian navigator—Giovanni da Verrazzano—and commissioned him to explore unknown latitudes in the western Atlantic in search of a northerly route to China. In 1524 the hundred-ton ship *La Dauphine* sailed with a crew of fifty aboard, intending to reach China by sea. If blocked by "a barrier of new land," Verrazzano would search for a "strait to penetrate to the Eastern Ocean."

After weathering a February storm "as violent as ever sailing man encountered," Verrazzano proceeded westward along the thirty-fourth degree of latitude until mid-March. Suddenly the "sweet fragrance" of large forests filled the ocean breeze, and "there appeared a new land which had never been seen before by any [European] man, either ancient or modern. At first it appeared to be rather low-

(Left) Theodore De Bry engraving of John White's painting of an Indian camp fire. N.C. State Archives.

Giovanni da Verrazzano (ca. 1480–ca. 1527). *Annual Report of the State Historian* (Albany: State of New York, 1916).

Cypress knees in a North Carolina swamp.

Dismal Swamp State Park, Camden County, shows how much of eastern North Carolina must have looked to the first settlers. Remaining today are some of the oldest ditches and canals, which were built in the hope of making the swampland productive.

lying; having approached to within a quarter of a league, we realized that it was inhabited, for huge fires had been built on the seashore."

Looking for China, the explorer had encountered what would later be North Carolina. His initial landfall was somewhere along the coast north of Cape Fear in what is now New Hanover County. But, like Columbus, Verrazzano searched for signs that he had reached some outer tip of Asia. He reported that the inhabitants "resemble the Orientals, particularly those from the farthest Sinarian regions" and that the ground was of a color that suggested gold. He noted "palms, laurel, cypress and other varieties of tree unknown in our Europe" in the fragrant forests he and his men had smelled from a hundred leagues off shore. "We think that they belong to the Orient by virtue of the surroundings, and that they are not without some kind of narcotic or aromatic liquor."

Like any newcomer in the early spring, Verrazzano was thoroughly charmed by the Cape Fear region. He named it "Forest of Laurels" and noted that it lay in the same latitude as spice-rich Damascus. He informed the king of France of the abundant game, the mild climate, the pure air, the gentle breezes, and the clear skies. "The seashore is completely covered with fine sand XV feet deep, which rises in the shape of small hills about fifty paces wide," he recounted. "Nearby we could see a stretch of country much higher than the sandy shore, with many beautiful fields and planes full of great forests, some sparse and some dense; and the trees have so many colors, and are so beautiful and delightful that they defy description."

Had *La Dauphine* arrived later in the year, the coastline might have been nearly deserted, for at that time the Cape Fear and Waccamaw Indians moved inland to harvest their crops and establish seasonal hunting camps near the numerous bay lakes in modern-day Columbus and Bladen counties. But in March the shore was alive with local and inland groups, coming together to fish after planting their spring crops. They welcomed the first European party to come ashore, showing them where to beach their boat and offering them food. They marveled at the small stature, pale skin, and elaborate clothing of the French sailors. Verrazzano set down the earliest written description of the residents of coastal Carolina:

> They go nude of everything except that at the private parts they wear some skins of little animals like martins, a girdle of fine grass woven with various tails of other animals which hang around the body as far as the knees; the rest nude; the head, likewise. Some wear certain garlands of feathers of birds. They are of dark color not much unlike the Ethiopians, and hair black and thick, and not very long, which they tie together back on the head in the shape of a little tail. As for the symmetry of the man,

they are well proportioned, of medium stature, and rather exceed us. In the breast they are broad, their arms well built, the legs and other parts of the body well put together. The eyes black and large, the glance intent and quick. They are not of much strength, in craftiness acute, agile and the greatest runners.

Sailing northeastward up the Carolina coast, Verrazzano resumed his search for the Pacific, and by the end of March he thought he had found it. On 25 March he anchored off Portsmouth Bank or Ocracoke Island and sent crewmen ashore to obtain fresh water. The land appeared to be "an isthmus a mile in width and about 200 long." Looking northwest across the isthmus from the rigging, crewmen gazed at open water stretching as far as the horizon. "We could see the eastern sea from the ship," Verrazzano recorded. "This is doubtless the one which goes around the tip of India, China, and Cathay."

The water in the distance was not the Pacific, but Pamlico Sound. A drive along Route 12 through the Cape Hatteras National Seashore today explains Verrazzano's mistake. Nowhere else on the eastern seaboard does such a wide stretch of water—more than twenty-five miles in places—separate barrier islands from the mainland coast. He named the isthmus "Verrazzania" and continued along the coast, "hoping all the time to find some strait or real promontory where the land might end to the north, and we could reach those blessed shores of Cathay."

The blessed shores of China eluded Verrazzano; he was killed by Caribs in the West Indies several years later. But his suggestion of a Carolina route to China endured for generations, largely through the work of his brother who, like Columbus's brother, was a mapmaker. The 1529 world map of Girolamo Verrazzano, which today survives in the Vatican library, shows Pamlico Sound stretching westward all the way to the Pacific. A note on the map beside Cape Hatteras reads: "From this Eastern Ocean one sees the Western Ocean."

North Carolina, in other words, was underwater as far as the Verrazzano brothers were concerned, and it remained that way on some European charts for almost a century. Maps made by the Englishmen John Dee and John White in the 1580s showed a huge bay, "The Sea of Verrazzano," stretching from Southern California to the Carolina coast. Early in the seventeenth century, the English settlers at Jamestown were actually supplied with prefabricated boats for a possible portage to the nearby Pacific. They were instructed to probe the coastal rivers and to look beyond the adjacent mountains for some quick access to the "East India Sea."

Verrazzano had put North America on the globe for Europeans, but taken North Carolina off. Where the Town Creek Indian Mound

John White painting of a North Carolina Indian in body paint. N.C. State Archives.

Sea oats on sand dunes at dawn.

The exact location cannot be known, but a highway marker on N.C. #107 suggests that de Soto's party entered North Carolina nearby.

stood, he imagined only a long finger of the Pacific. If he had been correct, all American history would be different, and Hawaiian cruise ships and Japanese freighters might be sailing westward regularly from New Bern and Edenton. But it was the fragrant forest with its numerous inhabitants, not the glistening waters of Pamlico Sound, which stretched beyond the western horizon. It would take generations for Europeans to come to understand what native Americans had known for centuries about the rich landscape of North Carolina.

The quest for an "Eastern Sea" had brought the French to North Carolina. Gold brought the Spanish. Though the vast wealth of the Aztec and Inca empires preoccupied most Spaniards in the New World, a few conquistadors hoped to find comparable riches in the interior of North America. While Coronado explored the southwest, Hernando de Soto led the hunt for treasure in the southeast. His army of six hundred soldiers plunged into the southern interior and became the first Europeans to see the southern Appalachian Range and encounter its Indian inhabitants.

In May 1539 de Soto landed near Tampa Bay. He had served under Pizarro in the conquest of Peru, and he now aspired to locate and subdue a similar empire of his own. He had received royal permission to "conquer and settle" the vast region north of Florida, including the right to build stone forts and import Negro slaves. His nine ships brought soldiers, servants, slaves, and camp followers, along with 220 horses, plus hogs, mules, and vicious Irish hounds.

The expedition northward took a full year. The soldiers lived off their expanding herd of hogs and food extorted from tribes along the way. Local Indians were commandeered by de Soto as burden bearers and locked in chains if they resisted. Others, forced to serve as guides, were thrown to the hounds if they displeased de Soto. By May 1540 the company had penetrated northward through modern-day Georgia and South Carolina to the Indian town of Xuala, "a village in a plain between two rivers" at the edge of the southern mountains.

Exactly how far north de Soto's expedition penetrated remains a mystery. Accepted judgments have put Xuala near the present-day intersection of the South Carolina, North Carolina, and Georgia borders, but some scholars now locate Xuala much farther north, between Marion and Old Fort in McDowell County. Whatever their exact point of departure, the Spaniards spent the last week of May crossing the high terrain of southeastern Appalachia. Mountain laurel, flaming azaleas and rhododendrons must have been coming into bloom. Except near Indian villages, the high forest of huge oak, poplar, hickory, and chestnut trees had never been cut over. Mile after mile of primeval woodlands appeared as they still do in the Joyce Kilmer Memorial Forest in Graham County.

Pushing over the steep ridges, the explorers soon encountered streams flowing north and west rather than south and east—they had crossed the Appalachian Divide. By June they had pressed into Tennessee and were moving on toward the banks of the Mississippi. A generation later, a smaller Spanish expedition under Captain Juan Pardo explored the region again, following a similar path and intending to open a pathway to the Mexican frontier as well as spread the gospel to the Indians.

The Indians encountered by Pardo's group in southern Appalachia were the Cherokees. (The word Cherokee derived from "Tsalagi," or "Tsaragi," meaning "cave people.") Their language stemmed from Iroquoian stock, and their ancestors had migrated south from beyond the Ohio River hundreds of years earlier. In the mid-sixteenth century they probably numbered well over twenty thousand persons, living in scores of widely dispersed villages. The rugged mountain terrain both isolated and protected the Lower Towns below the modern South Carolina border, the Middle Towns of Jackson and

Hernando de Soto (ca. 1500–42). Buckingham Smith, tr., *Narratives of the Career of Hernando de Soto in the Conquest of Florida . . .* (New York, 1866).

Turk's cap lily, Joyce Kilmer Memorial Forest, Nantahala National Forest, Graham County.

Macon counties, the Valley Towns of Clay and Cherokee counties, and the Overhill Towns of western Swain and Graham counties. Tribesmen hunted widely beyond these core settlements for deer and also buffalo, which were plentiful in the southeast until the eighteenth century. Agriculture in the fertile river valleys centered around corn, beans, sunflowers, and a variety of squashes, pumpkins, and gourds.

Economically self-sufficient and geographically protected, the Cherokees adapted to European colonization pressures. But their numbers were decimated by smallpox epidemics in the 1730s, and a century later the U.S. government forcibly removed the majority of the tribe to Oklahoma to make way for white land speculators. The descendants of those who remained now constitute the Eastern Band of Cherokees, living in and around the Qualla Boundary. At Oconaluftee, on U.S. 441 north of Cherokee, Swain County, a traditional village has been reconstructed and is open to visitors every summer. Though designed to portray a later period, the village is on a site that has been used for thousands of years.

Despite a half-century of overland Spanish exploration of the southeast, nothing was known of the Cherokees or of Spanish contact with them in Elizabethan England. There the idea of Verrazzano's Sea was still widely accepted. Sir Humphrey Gilbert, given royal permission to explore and settle the American coast, possessed a chart showing the vast gulf stretching from the Pacific to the Carolina Piedmont. When Gilbert was lost at sea in 1583, his half brother, Walter Raleigh, obtained the letters patent of his deceased relative and dispatched two barks to explore the region of Verrazzano's isthmus.

Leaving Plymouth on 27 April, Captains Philip Amadas and Arthur Barlow reached the Outer Banks on 13 July and claimed the land for Queen Elizabeth. Unlike Verrazzano, they located an inlet through the cape and were able to drop anchor in the sound near an island which "the Indians call Roanoak." After six weeks of exploration and trade, they carried back favorable reports and two Indians, Manteo and Wanchese, to Raleigh and Elizabeth. On 6 January 1585, when Raleigh was knighted by the Virgin Queen and given permission to call the land Virginia in her honor, plans were already under way for a permanent settlement.

The second expedition, under Sir Richard Grenville, sailed from Plymouth with seven ships in April and reached Ocracoke Inlet on 26 June. After two months of careful exploration aided by scientist Thomas Harriot and artist John White, Grenville returned to England with detailed maps, plus riches from a Spanish flagship he captured on the homeward crossing. He left behind 108 men, under Governor Ralph Lane, at a crude settlement called Fort Raleigh on Roanoke Island.

Stream in Joyce Kilmer Memorial Forest.

Highway markers at Highlands (Jackson County), Franklin (Macon County), Brasstown (Clay County), and Murphy (Cherokee County) suggest a possible route of the 1567 journey of Juan de Pardo.

American bison (buffalo). Mark Catesby, *The Natural History of Carolina, Florida, and the Bahama Islands*, vol. 2 (London, 1743).

Mark Catesby (1682–1749) was one of the many naturalists who visited America to record its flora and fauna. The result of his two visits (1712–19 and 1722–26) was his monumental *The Natural History of Carolina, Florida, and the Bahama Islands*. It contains 220 folio-sized, hand-colored etchings.

Visitors to Oconaluftee Village can meet artisans who still know how to hollow logs with fire to make canoes; weave baskets from dried oak, river cane, and honeysuckle; and create blowguns from cane stalks for hunting small game.

Sir Walter Raleigh (ca. 1552–1618). Engraving by H. Robinson from Federigo Zucchero's painting. N.C. State Archives.

Lane's band was plagued by internal rivalries, a preoccupation with gold, and a pathetic inability to find food in an abundant region. The arrival of Francis Drake's fleet in June 1586, bringing supplies and hundreds of liberated Indians and Africans taken in raids upon Spanish strongholds in the Caribbean, perhaps could have saved the colony. But a sudden storm scattered the smaller vessels near the entrance to Roanoke Sound. Lane and his men, who had alienated local Indians and killed several of their leaders weeks before, now gave up and sailed for England with Drake.

This was only the first of a string of losses and failures for the English. When Grenville arrived with promised supplies and reinforcements several weeks later, he found Roanoke deserted. Rather than regarrisoning Fort Raleigh with most of his four hundred men, he turned his fleet toward the Caribbean in search of Spanish prizes. He left behind only fifteen soldiers, who were never heard from again. In the spring of 1587 another settlement was planned. Led by John White and including women and children, the party of 110 left the English port of Plymouth in May to establish "The Cittie of Ra-

Fort Raleigh, Roanoke Island, Dare
County.

Sir Francis Drake (ca. 1540–96).
Engraving by S. Freeman. N.C. State
Archives.

legh in Virginea." They intended to settle on Chesapeake Bay, but
their pilot, eager for privateering in the Caribbean, left them at Roanoke instead. In mid-August Eleanor Dare, the wife of Ananias Dare
and daughter of John White, gave birth to the first American child
born to English parents. On 24 August she was christened "Virginia"
in honor of the newly claimed land, and several days later her grand-
father departed for England to procure much-needed supplies for
the colony.

John White's efforts to return to Roanoke the following spring
were foiled by the war between Spain and England and the threatened
invasion of the Spanish Armada. He did not reach the Outer Banks
again until 1590. A passage once existed north of modern Oregon
Inlet where Bodie Island later formed, and on 17 August a crew
sought to cross the shoals in a small boat. It was tossed about in the
heavy breakers and six sailors drowned in the surf. The survivors
made it to the north end of Roanoke Island after nightfall, anxious to
complete the long-awaited reunion. "We let fall our Grapnel neere
the shore, & sounded the trumpet with a Call, & afterwardes many
familiar English tunes of Songs, and called to them friendly; but we
had no answere."

Before White's departure three years earlier, the colonists had
discussed moving, and he had agreed with them that "they should not
faile to write or carve on the trees or posts of the dores the name of
the place where they should be seated." They had also agreed that
they would carve a Maltese cross above the place-name if they were
in distress. The next morning, White's men went ashore and found

the letters "CRO" carved on a tree in "faire Romane letters." Farther inland, overgrown with weeds and vines, they located the palisaded enclosure where the settlers had lived. A post to the right of the entrance had had the bark removed, "and 5. foote from the ground in fayre Capotall letters was graven CROATOAN without any crosse or sign of distress."

White assumed his colonists had elected to migrate southward to Croatoan Island (modern-day Ocracoke south of Cape Hatteras),

Artist's conception of the historic moment of John White's delayed return to Roanoke. North Carolina Collection, Louis R. Wilson Library, University of North Carolina, Chapel Hill.

20

led by their Indian associate, Manteo. "I had found a certain token of their safe being at Croatoan," White wrote, "which is the place where Manteo was borne, and the Savages of the Iland our friends." He hoped to find them there, but bad weather, the loss of vital cables and anchors, and the fears of the sailors, six of whom had already been killed in the rescue attempt, prevented White from searching further. He had found his own books and papers that he had left at Roanoke "rotten and spoyled with rayne" and a suit of armor "almost eaten through with rust." Because the hurricane season was approaching, he had no choice but to depart for England. On 24 October White's ship, having failed in its rescue attempt, "came in safetie, God be thanks, to an anker in Plymmouth."

It seems likely that at least some of the lost colony members did go south to live with the native people on the Outer Banks. In the mid-seventeenth century, the Hatteras Indians would migrate inland, like other small coastal groups at the same time, settling the area that is now Robeson County. It is quite possible, though not certain, that members of the Lumbee tribe now living in the Lumberton area may be descended in part from this Outer Banks contingent of Indians and English.

Some historians now believe that another contingent from Roanoke may have gone north to Chesapeake Bay, the colony's original destination, and settled among the Chesapeake Indians near Cape Henry. The Englishman William Strachey later claimed to have reports that Powhatan, advised by his counselors to destroy the Chesapeakes and the English living with them, had done so in 1607, at just the time that the Jamestown colonists arrived. The king of England had been informed, Strachey wrote, that Powhatan had "miserably slaughtered" the "men, women, and children of the first plantation at Roanoak . . . (who 20. and od yeeres had peacably lyved and intermixed with thos Savadges, and were out of his Territory)." The Jamestown colonists were specifically instructed to look for survivors from the lost colony, and two men sent to Roanoke Island in 1608 brought back crosses and letters of English origin, but no other news.

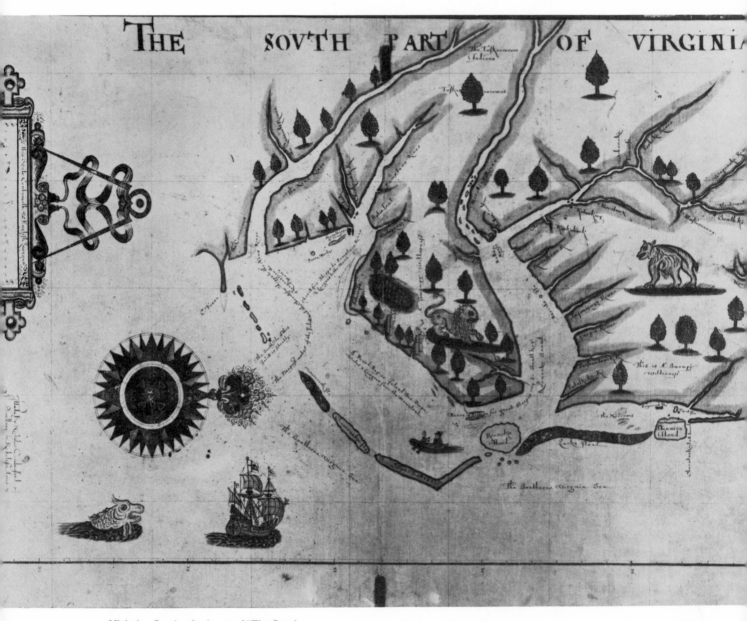

Nicholas Comberford map of "The South
Part of Virginia now the North Part of
Carolina," 1657. N.C. State Archives.
Reproduced through the courtesy of the
trustees of the National Maritime Mu-
seum, Greenwich, England.

Virginians in the Albemarle

After the failure of English settlement efforts at Roanoke, North Carolina Indians remained undisturbed for decades. When European intrusions finally did recur, they came not from the sea, but overland from the Virginia colony to the north. Indeed, the territory we now know as North Carolina was for years included in the tremendous Virginia Company land grant of 1606. The first permanent European settlements, in the far northeastern corner of North Carolina, were more an extension of the Virginia Company's colony at Jamestown than they were concerted efforts toward planting a new colony.

The northernmost stream feeding Albemarle Sound is the Chowan River, flowing south out of Virginia through modern Gates, Hertford, and Chowan counties. Its westernmost tributary is the Meherrin, entering near present-day Murfreesboro, where the Chowanoc Indian town of Ramashonoc once stood. The Blackwater River intersects the Chowan from the north, after flowing parallel to the James less than twenty miles southwest of Jamestown. Just as an expedition from Roanoke led by Ralph Lane had penetrated up the Chowan River in 1585, now Englishmen began to penetrate down the Blackwater and the Chowan toward Albemarle Sound.

As early as 1608 Captain John Smith sent two explorers from Jamestown into what would become North Carolina. Instructed to search for survivors of the Roanoke settlement, the two woodsmen probed about the Chowan River region and then returned. A year later, in May 1609, Virginia Governor Sir Thomas Gates received instructions from the proprietors of the Virginia Company, who financed and managed the company's affairs from England. They urged him to pursue a settlement on the Chowan River, where he would find abundant "grasse silke" and would be "neere Rich Coppermines." In 1610 an expedition set out for "parts of the Chowanok," but no records of the excursion survive.

More than a decade passed before Virginians again ventured into the North Carolina swamplands. At last John Pory, former secretary of the Virginia colony, set out for the Chowan River in February 1622. In his sermon of 18 April, the Reverend Patrick Copland reported that Pory had passed through a "great forest of Pynes 15. or 16. myle broad and above 60. mile long." The pines, he ventured, would "serve well for Masts for Shipping, and for pitch and tarre." Copland described the land Pory had found as "a fruitfull Countrie blessed with abundance of Corne, reaped twise a yeere." Echoing the proprietors' earlier view, he claimed to know of "Copper Mines"

To raise sufficient funds to finance another attempt at English colonization in the New World, James I in 1606 chartered the Virginia Company of London, a joint-stock company of merchants who hoped to make fortunes in mining and the Indian trade.

and "a great deale of silke grasse" in the region.

Although interest in the North Carolina region ran high in the years following Pory's excursion, no settlement attempts reached farther than the counties of Surry, Isle of Wight, and Nansemond, on the south shore of the James. Then, toward the middle of the seventeenth century, Virginia's steep mortality rate—caused by disease, Indian wars, and inadequate food and housing—began to decline. The colony's population grew at an unprecedented rate. In 1644, when several hundred colonists lost their lives in the last major effort of tidewater Indians to reclaim their land, Virginia's combined white and black population was around eight thousand. By 1653 it was fourteen thousand. And by 1662 it had probably topped twenty-five thousand. As her population expanded, Virginia's supply of land grew short. Interest in the region to the south mounted and exploration intensified. Unable to move west because of powerful Indian tribes, landless Virginians looked increasingly to the Albemarle frontier for the farms they could not acquire at home.

Virginians heading southward left behind a society irreversibly committed to the production of tobacco. In fact, Virginia's commitment to this single crop was in large part what led to her "shortage" of land. Every year hundreds of indentured servants, bound to a period of unpaid labor in exchange for passage to the New World, completed their terms of service and became freedmen. Like their former masters, these freedmen sought their fortunes in tobacco.

To the established planters, the sudden abundance of freedmen and the steady arrival of European immigrants posed a serious economic threat. As freedmen and new investors acquired land, tobacco production increased and the crop's market value inevitably dropped. Freedmen now competed with their former masters, and the supply of tobacco could not be restricted in order to keep prices high. Access to farmland diminished rapidly as wealthy planters began buying all the land they could, even purchasing the head rights of poorer settlers so that they could claim more acreage in the future. It was not long before most of the prime land lay in the hands of a few well-to-do owners.

As the grip on coastal farmlands tightened, driving up prices, ex-servants found it increasingly difficult to purchase land. Many gave up hope and returned to the land of their masters as renters. Others pushed westward up the river valleys to the backcountry frontiers. But they found themselves too far from the coastal ports and too close to local Indian tribes, as the events of Bacon's Rebellion in the 1670s revealed. Still others chose to migrate southward.

By 1655, in the area east of the Chowan River and south of the Great Dismal Swamp, North Carolina had her first permanent English settlers. Robert Brodman, a carpenter, had spent five months building a combination house and trading post on the southwestern bank of the Pasquotank River for Virginian Nathaniel Batts. Batts had already visited the area and established trade with local Indians. On 24 September 1660, five years after moving to the area, Batts purchased the land he lived on from its previous residents. In the first North Carolina land grant on record, King Kiscutanewh of the Weapemeoc tribe ceded to Batts, "for a valuable Consideration in hand received, viz &: all ye land on ye southwest side of Pascotank River, from ye mouth of ye s^d. River to ye head of new Begin Creeke, to have & to hold to him & his heires for Ever."

Others soon followed Batts to the promise of the Albemarle. One year after Batts received his grant, Kilcocanen, king of Yeopim, deeded to colonist George Durant "a Parcell of Land Lying & Being on Roanoke Sound & on a River Called By y^e. Name of Perquimans Which Isueth out of the North Side of the aforesaid Sound." Durant's Neck, in Perquimans County today, is a modern reminder of George Durant's settlement.

Along the banks of the Pasquotank, Perquimans, and Chowan rivers, migrants from Virginia found acres of arable land. The region, however, was not vacant; it had been settled and used for centuries. The incoming settlers all had to bargain with local Indians for the soil to plant on, just as Nathaniel Batts and George Durant had done. Sometimes they paid the Indians "a valuable consideration of satisfaction" in return for their land; other times they paid nothing at all and risked the consequences.

Many of these land transactions were founded on misunderstandings between the Indians and the English. For most southeastern tribes, the mere use of a plot of land established individual property rights. When use ceased, the land could be reclaimed by another. Europeans, however, saw no such connection between rights and use. Land was a commodity to be bought and sold. While the settlers who "acquired" Indian land undoubtedly assumed the transaction to be permanent, the Indians may have assumed it to be a temporary one based on their own traditional values.

Indian land was certainly in high demand. The North Carolina forest was known for its numerous "natural" meadows that could be quickly and easily turned to cultivation. John Lawson described the Carolina woods at the turn of the century: " . . . one part bearing great Timbers, others being Savanna's or natural Meads, where no Trees grow for several Miles, adorn'd by Nature with a pleasant Verdure, and beautiful Flowers, frequent in no other Places, yielding abundance of Herbage for Cattle, Sheep, and Horses." A newcomer in search of pasture and farmland could want little more.

But what John Lawson saw as the work of nature was often the work of man. Here, as elsewhere in the eastern woodlands, many of the "natural" meadows had actually been cleared by Indians years before. On colonial maps they were occasionally designated as "Indian

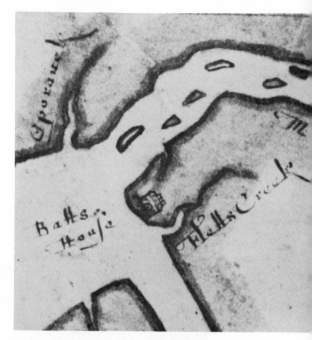

Detail of the Comberford map showing Nathaniel Batts's house. The dwelling Bodman built for Batts was twenty feet square with two rooms and a chimney.

George Fox, the Quakers' founder, traveled through the Albemarle in 1672 and met Nathaniel Batts, whom he described as a "rude, desperate man. He asked me about a woman in Cumberland, who, he said, he was told, had been healed by our prayers and laying on of hands, after she had been long sick, and given over by the physicians: he desired to know the certainty of it." Saunders, ed., *Colonial Records*, vol. 1.

North Carolina Coastal Plain.

John Brickell, despite much borrowing from earlier authors, including Lawson, made some original observations and added specific details in his *Natural History of North Carolina*: "Here are in several Places large Savannas, beautiful to behold, which at certain Seasons, appear at a distance like so many Pleasure Gardens, being intermixt with a variety of Spontaneous Flowers of various Colours, such as the Tulip, Trumpet-flower, Princess-feather, and several others, with great quantities of Grass on them, but of a coarser and stronger Nature than up the Rivers, where there is mostly Clover to be met with, notwithstanding Horses and other Cattle feed very well on the former, and are fat, strong, and fit for Labour, most Seasons of the Year."

old fields."

James Adair, who traded and worked among southeastern Indians for over thirty-five years, observed their slow but efficient method of stripping a ring of bark from the trunk to stop the flow of sap so that huge trees died and eventually toppled. "Now, in the first clearing of their plantations," Adair explained, "they only bark the large timber, cut down the saplings and underwood, and burn them in heaps; as the suckers shoot up, they chop them off close by the stump, of which they make fires to deaden the roots, till in time they decay." Thus, even without the added clearing power of metal axes, saws, and mattocks, "the contented natives got convenient fields in a matter of time." Because Indian farmers rotated fields, not crops, large tracts of land stood uncultivated for lengthy periods of time. Such seemingly abandoned land appeared ideal to the arriving settlers.

Naturally, the commercial crop the settlers planted in these fields was tobacco. They soon found, however, that, because of obstacles of geography, North Carolina tobacco rarely yielded the profits of Virginia tobacco. The Outer Banks and the shoals of the Albemarle Sound prevented heavy commercial vessels from reaching Carolina's shores safely; as a result, farmers could not ship their tobacco directly to England. Instead, they had to haul their harvest by land to Virginia before it could be shipped overseas.

Carrying tobacco to Virginia was no small problem. In the settlement's early years, no roads existed between Virginia and the Albemarle. A map made in 1657 bears the simple inscription "This is A Swampy wilderness" across the area north of Albemarle Sound where the Great Dismal Swamp lay squarely in the path of travelers. George Fox, the founder of the Quaker faith, who visited North Carolina in 1672, described his route as "full of great bogs and swamps; so that we were commonly wet to the knees, and lay abroad a-nights in the woods by a fire." The enormous cost of overland transit, combined with the export tax resulting from the Navigation Acts, was nearly prohibitive.

Finally, in 1663 Charles II, recently "restored" to the English throne, formally granted the Province of Carolina—from present-day Florida north to the Albemarle Sound region, and from the Atlantic Ocean west to the Pacific—to eight favored courtiers. By removing the Albemarle from Virginia's jurisdiction, the charter gave political definition to the geographic obstacles between the two regions. From 1679 to 1731 Virginia statutes prohibited the importation and reexportation of Albemarle tobacco through the northern colony's ports. The Virginians claimed the North Carolina product was inferior, but they were perhaps more worried about the rising competition and falling prices as tobacco exports climbed.

Some early Carolina planters evaded these restrictions by shipping their tobacco illegally. North Carolina's treacherous coastal wa-

A traveler described the Dismal Swamp: "The color of the water is a deep red, occasioned by the roots of the trees through which it passes; but it is perfectly clear, the taste by no means disagreeable, and very wholesome. Labouring people who reside near swamps, drink it in preference to spring water, attributing to its virtue the prevention of agues and bilious fevers. It is of a diuretic quality, and those who drink it are generally healthy, while others, at a distance from the swamps, in the fall of the year, are suffering under those complaints." Janson, *The Stranger in America*.

Colonial wharf. Detail from Fry-Jefferson map of "The Most Inhabited Parts of Virginia . . ." 1751. N.C. State Archives.

Newbold-White House, S.R. #1336, off U.S. #17 bypass west of Hertford, Perquimans County.

Table from the Albemarle, 1710–30. Courtesy Museum of Early Southern Decorative Arts.

terways made the colony an ideal base for pirates and smugglers. It was not long before traders from New England discovered the profits to be made in North Carolina tobacco. Using shallow-draft ships, these traders carried numerous loads of tobacco from the Albemarle region to the northern colonies and Newfoundland to evade the Navigation Acts. In 1673, however, England's Plantation Duty Act imposed customs duties on intercolonial shipping. This resulted in more illegal exports, and would later give rise to considerable political turmoil within North Carolina.

By 1663 the immigrant population of the tobacco-growing Albemarle region had passed five hundred. Scores of Virginians moved southward annually. The Newbold-White House, which stands in present-day Perquimans County, dates from this early period of migration from Virginia. The first European inhabitants of the site were among those visited by George Fox after his swampy trek of 1672. The house itself stands one-and-a-half stories tall on the west bank of the Perquimans River. Built of bricks made from local clay, it may be the oldest surviving brick home in North Carolina. Some historians believe the house was built as early as 1664, although others say it dates from about 1720.

The first probable owner of the Newbold-White House, a Quaker and justice of the General Court named Joseph Scott, did not own the land on which it stands until 1684. He had undoubtedly lived there for over a decade before the 640-acre grant became official. Scott shared the house with his family and two indentured servants: an Indian man named Alexander and a white man named John Browning. When Scott died in 1685, his son Joshua inherited the property. But Joshua, who served as justice of the Albemarle County court, only survived his father by three months. His widow soon remarried and remained in the house with her second husband, Thomas Blount. Although he was a carpenter, metalworker, and shipbuilder by trade, Blount also held numerous public offices. He was justice of the General Court, justice of the Chowan Precinct Court, captain of the militia, and vestryman of the Chowan Parish.

Clearly, his new wife's solid dwelling further enhanced Thomas Blount's status and set him apart from less fortunate parishioners. Both the home and its inhabitants were exceptionally secure, yet the story of the early site still remains difficult to piece together. Much of that history must be reconstructed not from documents, but from the structure of the house and the layout of its surrounding grounds.

For example, evidence reveals that an animal pen stood near the Newbold-White House. Animal husbandry in the Albemarle was limited primarily to hogs and cattle, which were penned occasionally but usually allowed to graze freely in surrounding woods and meadows. (In so doing, livestock often did considerable damage to unfenced Indian cornfields. This would prove a constant source of tension be-

According to Brickell, house furniture in North Carolina in the 1730s consisted of "Pewter, Brass, Tables, Chairs, which are imported here commonly from England. The better sort have tolerable Quantities of Plate, with other convenient, ornamental, and valuable Furniture." The inhabitants of the Newbold-White House were of the "better sort."

Interior, Newbold-White House.

tween Indians and newly arrived settlers.) On occasion, settlers raised sheep, and these animals also may have been kept in the Newbold-White animal pen.

Late in the year, when the weather was cold and the animals were at their fattest, Carolinians slaughtered their livestock. After slaughtering, Newbold-White House owners, or more likely their

"The Southern pine woods hog, which ranged wild in the woods at all seasons, developed fleetness of foot, coarse, large bones, and a thick, hard coat." Ernest L. Bogart, *The Economic History of the United States* (New York, 1907).

William Byrd of Virginia saw inefficiency in the way livestock was managed: "Both Cattle and Hogs ramble in the Neighbouring Marshes and Swamps, where they maintain themselves the whole Winter long, and are not fetch'd home till the Spring. Thus these Indolent Wretches, during one half of the Year, lose the Advantage of the Milk of their Cattle, as well as their Dung, and many of the poor Creatures perish in the Mire, into the Bargain, by this ill Management."

Brickell described the houses he saw in North Carolina: "Their Houses are built after two different ways; viz. the most substantial Planters generally use Brick, and Lime, which is made of Oyster-shells, for there are no Stones to be found proper for that purpose, but near the Mountains; the meaner Sort erect with Timber, the outside with Clap-Boards, the Roofs of both Sorts of Houses are made with Shingles, and they generally have Sash Windows, and affect large and decent Rooms with good Closets, as they do a most beautiful Prospect by some noble River or Creek."

servants, cured the meat in a smokehouse. The smoke of burning hardwood preserved beef, venison, fish, and other meats while imparting a unique smoky flavor. Considerable quantities of meat could thus be stored for year-round consumption. Meat evidently made up a substantial portion of the colonial North Carolinian's diet. "These People live so much upon Swine's flesh," an arrogant William Byrd of Virginia exclaimed, "that it . . . makes them extremely hoggish in their Temper, & many of them seem to Grunt rather than to speak."

Undoubtedly the most important cultivated foodstuff was corn, the high-yield Indian grain that Europeans readily adopted throughout the New World. "Had it not been for the Fruitfulness of this Species," wrote the English explorer John Lawson in Carolina, "it would have proved very difficult to have settled some of the Plantations in America." For settlers in the Albemarle, corn became the staple grain to be ground into meal and baked into bread. But planters also grew garden vegetables to supplement the usual fare of bread and meat. Some planted herbs as well for seasoning and medicinal purposes. One of the earliest structures at the Newbold-White House probably was a root cellar to protect tubers and other vegetables from the humid summer heat.

In the early years of the Newbold-White House and of the Albemarle settlement, these food sources did not prove so reliable as they might at first seem. Violent storms, hurricanes, and droughts destroyed crops and livestock alike in the four years from 1667 to 1671. Peter Carteret, who served as governor from 1670 to 1672, reported that in 1667 a hurricane "destroyed both corne & tob: blew downe the roof of the great hogg howse." In 1668 first drought and then torrential rains ruined crops. Another hurricane struck in 1669 which, according to Carteret, "destroyed what tob was out . . . & spoiled most of the corne this yeare." The following year, a twenty-

30

four-hour hurricane blew down trees, houses, and the "hogg howse." Conditions were so bad that Carteret proclaimed there was bound "to bee a famine amongst us."

Only an exceptionally solid structure like the Newbold-White House could survive such repeated storms, and it is clear that the substantial twenty-by-forty-foot house, built of bricks laid in Flemish bond, is hardly representative of early North Carolina homes. More characteristic was the "20 foot dwelling howse" Peter Carteret found awaiting him on Colleton Island in February 1664. Three years later, a hurricane "carried away the frame & boards of two howses." Wood, not bricks, remained the basic building material, and as tar became a staple of the colony it was used to weatherproof local dwellings. When William Logan visited the colony in 1745, he reported: "The Common peoples houses here are in generall tarr[d] all over to preserve y[m] instead of Painting & all have Wooden Chimneys which I admire do not catch fire oftener than they do." Because most inhabitants of the Albemarle frontier had only limited access to capital, labor, and materials, their houses were probably like the simple ones Carteret and Logan described.

Unlike the residents of the Newbold-White House, the inhabitants of these simple wooden homes were people who could not get by or get ahead in neighboring Virginia. Escaped slaves as well as freedmen migrated southward. "It is certain," wrote Virginia colonist William Byrd, who surveyed the boundary between Virginia and Carolina in 1728, that "many Slaves Shelter themselves in this Obscure part of the World, nor will any of their righteous Neighbors discover them." Most early migrants—black or white—left little behind and brought little with them. They lacked the assets to establish large plantations and were isolated from the deep-water ports around which large fortunes could be quickly built. But, if their situation was remote, it was also secure, and an independent community began to emerge around Albemarle Sound.

William Gordon, an Anglican missionary, described living conditions in North Carolina in 1709: "Here [Perquimans] and in Chowan the ways of living are much alike; both are equally destitute of good water, most of that being brackish and muddy; they feed generally upon salt pork, and sometimes upon beef, and their bread of Indian corn which they are forced for want of mills to beat; and in this they are so careless and uncleanly that there is but little difference between the corn in the horse's manger and the bread on their tables: so that with such provisions and such drink (for they have no beer), in such a hot country, you may easily judge, sir, what a comfortable life a man must lead; not but that the place is capable of better things, were it not overrun with sloth and poverty." Saunders, ed., *Colonial Records*, vol. 1.

St. Thomas Church, Bath, Beaufort
County, was begun in 1734. "We are
now building at our own proper Costs a
small Church (being the only one in the
whole province)" the vestry and church-
wardens wrote in 1734. Angley, "History of St. Thomas Episcopal Church."

Town-Planting

As colonists from Virginia first moved overland into the Albemarle region, other Englishmen and their African slaves began arriving by sea to establish settlements farther south. In the five years between 1662 and 1668, two separate expeditions would attempt to build towns in the Cape Fear region of North Carolina. Both would fail. For the remainder of the seventeenth century, and for the first quarter of the eighteenth, the European settlement of North Carolina would take place as it had started—from the north. As land ran short in the Albemarle, colonists moved into the Pamlico. Population centers developed. Before long, towns—Edenton, Bath, New Bern, and Beaufort—would dot the Carolina coastline.

In mid-August 1662 a tiny expedition left the Massachusetts Bay Colony for Carolina, its sights set on "the discovery of Cape Feare and more South parts of Florida." Sponsored by merchants calling themselves the "committee for Cape Faire at Boston," the ship *Adventure* and its crew returned home with good news. The Cape Fear region abounded with "upland fields . . . for Catle," and "abundance of vast meadows" for "multitudes of farms." Of course it also had swamps, but even they were "laden with varieties of great Oakes and other trees of all Sorts." The explorers noted few mosquitoes or rattlesnakes.

Encouraged by this promising description, a group of hopeful migrants sailed to Cape Fear with a supply of hogs and cattle early in 1663. Within months, the Puritan adventurers had had their fill. They soon returned to Boston, leaving their livestock behind. Tacked to a post they left a note intended for "the great discouragement of all those that should hereafter come into these parts to settle." The exact reasons for their own discouragement remain unknown.

In the same year, the proprietors received the charter to Carolina. All of these wealthy aristocrats had other interests in the expanding web of English mercantilism. Some were owners of the Royal Africa Company, and many had connections to the Caribbean island of Barbados. Sir Anthony Ashley Cooper, for instance, had invested in a Barbadian plantation in the 1640s. Sir John Colleton, described by some as "a Barbadian financier," had become a sizable planter with ties to the governor of the island. So it is hardly surprising that one of the earliest efforts to establish plantations at Cape Fear came from Barbados.

The situation on Barbados helped motivate such settlement. Barbadians, like coastal Virginians, were running out of land. During

In 1711 a New Bern settler, Christen Janzen, in a letter home described the area: "It is almost wholly forest, with indescribably beautiful cedar wood, poplars, oaks, beech, walnut and chestnut trees. . . . There is sassafras also, and so many other fragrant trees that I cannot describe the hundredth part. Cedar is red like the most beautiful cherry and smells better than the finest juniper. They are, commonly, as well as the other trees, fifty to sixty feet below the limbs." Todd, ed., *Founding of New Bern.*

"God preserve Carolina and the Lords Proprietors" says the obverse of this 1694 gold coin, N.C. Museum of History Collection. N.C. State Archives.

Lawson described the wild grapes he saw: "These refuse no Ground, swamp or dry, but grow plentifully on the Sand-Hills along the Sea-Coast, and elsewhere, and are great Bearers. I have seen near twelve Bushels upon one Vine of the black sort. Some of these, when thoroughly ripe, have a very pretty vinous Taste and eat very well, yet are glutinous. . . . Being removed by the Slip or Root, they thrive well in our Gardens, and make pleasant Shades."

the decades after 1660, as a profitable sugar economy based on race slavery became entrenched, the island's wealthiest planters steadily enlarged their holdings. By 1680 less than 7 percent of all landowners claimed over 50 percent of the land and devoted their massive estates entirely to cash crop production. The island's timber reserve for boiling sugar and making barrels was nearly exhausted, and the local supply of foodstuffs and other staples was inadequate for the expanding work force. It seemed only natural to turn to Carolina, a land well endowed with woods and fertile soil.

Like the Puritans before them, the Barbadians hired Captain William Hilton to undertake preliminary explorations. On 10 August 1663 Hilton once again sailed for the Cape Fear River. On his return to Barbados, he presented a glowing description much like his report to the Puritans a year before. The land, he said, was "as good land and as well timbered as any we have seen in any other part of the world, sufficient to accommodate thousands of our English nation, and lying commodiously by the said river's side." He stressed to the wine-loving planters that grape vines grew everywhere.

The Barbadians, and likewise the Carolina proprietors, were easily convinced. Representatives of the proprietors drew up a set of proposals designed to encourage the settlement of plantations at Cape Fear. The proprietors offered a "head right," or grant of land, for every person transported to the new settlement. Thus the more laborers a planter sent to Carolina, the more land he received in return. The laborers could be men or women, European or African, enslaved or free. Knowing that black slaves had been present in Barbados for a generation, the Carolina proprietors offered "To the Owner of every Negro-Man or Slave, brought thither to settle within the first year, twenty acres; and for every Woman-Negro or Slave, ten acres of Land."

Even before they had completed arrangements with the proprietors, a party of Barbadians set sail for Cape Fear. Although the exact size of this party is unclear, it seems certain that many of the colonists were indentured white servants or African slaves. The settlers landed on the west bank of the Cape Fear River on 26 May 1664. They selected a site for the settlement of Charles Town about twenty miles upstream, two miles east of Town Creek in present-day Brunswick County.

A series of mishaps soon threatened the life of the colony. Another party of settlers arrived in 1665 after a trying voyage entailing a shipwreck and the loss of much-needed food, clothing, and other supplies. In desperation the Charles Town colonists sent a sloop to Virginia for provisions. On her return the boat, "being ready by reason of her extreme rottenness in her timbers to Sinke," ran aground at Cape Lookout. The provisions were lost. Meanwhile, relations between colonists and the Cape Fear Indians had deteriorated. In "actuall warre with the natives," colonists killed Indian warriors, seized their children, and sold them into slavery. Unable to match the firepower of the English guns, the natives crippled the settlement by stealing its livestock. By late 1666 departing colonists outnumbered new arrivals.

Frantic efforts by the proprietors and Barbadian planters to save the colony were to no avail. No more were men drawn by the promotional claim of "good houses" and "good forts." Nor did the promoters beguile many a "Maid or single Woman" with the promise of a "Golden Age"—"for if they be but Civil, and under 50 years of Age, some honest Man or other, will purchase them for their Wives." The fact was, the governor of the colony reported in September 1666, "that thes Settlements have beene made and upheld by Negroes and without constant supplies of them cannot subsist." But more unfree labor was not to be had—it was too profitable in the Caribbean to be spared for Cape Fear. By the summer of 1667 the colony was deserted and the Indians had reclaimed their land. Until 1725 Europeans made no further attempts to settle at Cape Fear.

In the interim, the region's political status would change considerably. In 1689 the proprietors appointed Philip Ludwell as governor not just of the Albemarle, but of all Carolina "north and east of Cape Feare." In so doing, they established North Carolina and South Carolina as separate political units—a distinction that remains to this day.

Despite the failure of the best-laid plans of Boston Puritans and Barbadian proprietors, land-hungry settlers continued to stream into North Carolina. From Virginia, colonists pressed southward down the coast, past Pamlico Sound, across the Neuse, on to the North and Newport rivers. Although most of the European settlers were yeoman farmers, the colony began to attract nonfarmers as well. Settlements at the mouths of rivers became small towns, and soon housed the workshops of cobblers and tanners, tailors and blacksmiths. Lawyers and officials opened offices. Merchants established stores and provided imported goods—in limited variety—for townsfolk and for farmers from the interior.

The earliest of Carolina's immigrants to settle in a town clustered in the village of Roanoke—present day Edenton—on the northwestern shore of Albemarle Sound. The commercial center of the Albemarle, Roanoke became the region's political center as well in 1710, when it became the capital of "that part of the Province of Carolina that lies North and East of Cape Fear." Renamed Queen Ann's Town in 1715, the town acquired its final name in 1722 when it was incorporated as Edenton, honoring the memory of Governor Charles Eden.

The town of Edenton, in the first region of North Carolina to be permanently settled by Europeans, contains some of the colony's

William Byrd made the following observation about Edenton in 1728: "They may be 40 or 50 Houses, most of them Small, and built without Expense. A Citizen here is counted extravagant, if he has Ambition enough to aspire to a Brick-chimney. Justice herself is but indifferently Lodged, the Court-House having much the Air of a Common Tobacco-House."

Chowan County Courthouse (1767), Edenton.

Interior, Chowan County Courthouse.

In 1752, when Bishop Spangenberg and the other Moravians were in North Carolina seeking land for settlement, they spent time in Edenton equipping themselves for their journey into the backcountry. Spangenberg found Francis Corbin very helpful: "He is very busy, being not only My Lord Granville's Agent but also Judge of the Court of Admiralty and of the Supreme Court, not to speak of other employment; however, almost every day I have spent some hours with him, which was to my advantage. He is a walking encyclopedia concerning North Carolina affairs, is capable, polite, and very obliging." Fries, ed., *Records of the Moravians*, vol. 2.

oldest public buildings and private residences. The first courthouse, located where the village green is today, was completed in 1719. By the time of the American Revolution, the building had been replaced by a sturdy, Georgian-style brick structure. Constructed next to the green in 1767, the new building is still open to the public. In 1725, only six years after the first courthouse had been constructed, a wealthy sea captain named Richard Sanderson had the elegant Cupola House built on Broad Street. It derives its name from the octagonal cupola crowning the roof. Francis Corbin, the land agent of Lord Granville, purchased the house in 1756.

While Edenton was establishing itself as the commercial and political center of the Albemarle region, land-hungry settlers from Virginia were continuing their migration southward. Small commercial and political centers soon grew up in the Pamlico region. The earliest of the Pamlico centers was Bath Town. Incorporated in 1706, Bath is situated in present-day Beaufort County on the north bank of the Pamlico River. One of the first residents and commissioners of Bath was explorer-naturalist John Lawson. In February 1701, when Lawson completed his "thousand miles travel" through the Carolinas,

(Upper) Cupola House (1725), Edenton, Chowan County. *(Lower)* View from the cupola.

he emerged from the backwoods within twenty miles of the town's future location. Lawson may have chosen the site for Bath Town; it is certain that he helped lay out the town before its incorporation.

In the year before Bath was incorporated, the English Parliament passed a law that gave an important new stimulus to the economy of colonial North Carolina. Wary of continued dependence on Sweden and Finland for naval stores, English mercantilists hoped the Naval Stores Act of 1705 would wean the British shipbuilding industry from its dependency upon products from the Baltic. Naval stores—tar, turpentine, pitch, and hemp—were essential materials for the construction and maintenance of wooden sailing ships. For a strong seagoing nation with growing concerns in global commerce, such supplies were of no small importance. By paying premiums on naval stores imported from British colonies, Parliament hoped to encourage production in North America. The act offered substantial subsidies of £ 4 per ton on tar and pitch, £ 6 per ton on hemp.

For North Carolina merchants and planters, the bounties meant that the trade in tar and pitch was suddenly profitable. Although exports of naval stores would be highest in the Cape Fear region,

37

A bedroom (above) and the kitchen (below), Palmer-Marsh House (before 1758), Bath, Beaufort County.

where production was closely tied to the availability of slaves, all of North Carolina's ports participated in the trade. Even at Port Bath, which handled fewer naval stores than any other North Carolina port, merchants were able to amass sizable fortunes through the trade in the mid-eighteenth century. One such merchant, emblem of the lucrative and lively commercial enterprise that the Naval Stores Act made possible, was Michael Coutanch. His spacious house—today called the Palmer-Marsh House—survives in Historic Bath and identifies Coutanch as one of the wealthiest residents of the county. Tradition has it that Coutanch first sold his wares from a storeroom on the ground floor of the house. His ship, the *New Bern*, made regular runs to Liverpool carrying hundreds of barrels of North Carolina tar. For the return trip, the *New Bern* took on retail merchandise for sale in Coutanch's North Carolina stores.

In 1706, while John Lawson and other colonists were founding Bath Town on the Pamlico, settlements began springing up on the south side of the Neuse. During the next two years, newcomers moved farther southeast toward Cape Lookout, into modern Carteret County, and constructed houses on the North and Newport rivers.

Between the two rivers, a narrow spit of land held obvious promise as a seaport. Well protected and easily accessible to the sea, the unnamed inlet drew the attention of the deputy surveyor of North Carolina in 1713, who drafted a "Plan of Beaufort Towne" that year. Named for the Duke of Beaufort, one of the eight Carolina proprietors, the town today bears much resemblance to its original design, and its street names—Queen, Ann, Orange—honor still the monarchs of the era.

Despite Beaufort's well-laid plans, the town grew little in its early years. North Carolina Governor George Burrington wrote in 1731 that Beaufort had acquired "little success & scarce any inhabitants." A French visitor in 1765 found Beaufort "a Small village not above 12 houses." The "inhabitants seem miserable, they are very lasy and Indolent, they live mostly on fish and oisters, which they have in great plenty."

Indeed, for Beaufort and other coastal Carolina communities, the easy bounty of the sea put fish on the table and cash on the barrel. To naturalist and traveler John Lawson, the red drum caught off the coast provided not only "good firm meat" but an excellence of taste "beyond all the Fish I ever met." "People go down and catch as many barrels full as they please with Hook and Line." Palatable and abun-

Governor William Tryon described Robert Palmer's hospitality: "He had a very excellent House and Plantation at Bath which I often resided in with my family being Hospitably entertained by him." Cross, "Historical Research Report."

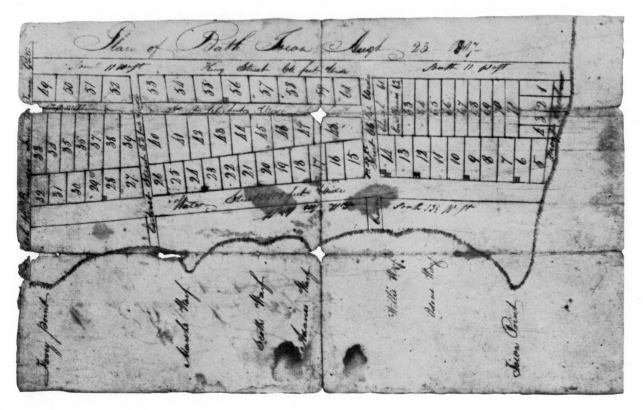

Plan of the Town of Bath. James R. Hoyle's 1807 copy of a 1766 original by John Forbis, deputy surveyor. N.C. State Archives.

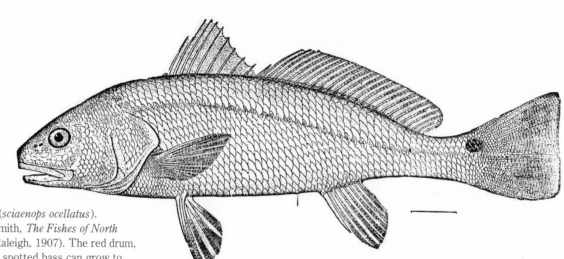

Red Drum (*sciaenops ocellatus*).
Hugh M. Smith, *The Fishes of North Carolina* (Raleigh, 1907). The red drum, red-fish, or spotted bass can grow to five feet in length and seventy-five pounds, but the usual catch weighs about five pounds.

"The Red Drum is a large Fish much bigger than the Blue-Fish. The Body of this is good firm Meat, but the Head is beyond all the Fish I ever met withal for an excellent Dish. We have greater Numbers of these Fish than any other sort." Lawson, *A New Voyage to Carolina*.

Joseph Bell House (1767), Beaufort, Carteret County. N.C. State Archives.

dant, great quantities of drumfish were "salted up and transported" from Beaufort "to the other Colonies, that are bare of Provisions."

Many residents of colonial Beaufort worked in either the fishing or forest products industries. Others labored at a trade that was actually a combination of both: shipbuilding. In 1713 George Bell, whose well-to-do family had first settled in Currituck County in the Albemarle, arranged to train two servants "in ye building of Vessells." Before long, residents of Harkers Island, just east of Beaufort, became known for their finely crafted boats. Even today the skill of Harkers Island boat builders is widely respected. By 1811 an observer in Beaufort would report: "The principle trade carried on here is Ship building in which they have acquired a very considerable reputation both on account of the solidity of the materials & the Judgement and Skill of their workmen as well as in modelling [and] in compleating their Vessels."

Shipbuilding set Beaufort apart from other early Carolina towns, but by the mid-eighteenth century some of the largest fortunes there, as elsewhere along the coast, were being amassed by purchasing a non-European work force and collecting the profits of their agricultural labor. Joseph Bell, for example, who had a substantial two-and-a-half-story house constructed in about 1767, did not labor at shipbuilding or fishing but instead maintained a large plantation operated by enslaved Africans. The red painted siding and fine furnishings of his Beaufort home clearly reflect the wealth he accumulated. Like the Palmer-Marsh House in Bath and the Cupola House in Edenton, the Joseph Bell House in Beaufort provided comforts far beyond those found in the dwellings of most Carolinians.

Edenton, Bath, and Beaufort were settled primarily by Virginians and other colonists migrating south. One Pamlico town was established in a very different manner. In 1710 over four hundred immigrants from the Swiss and German Palatinate arrived in the Pamlico to establish the town of New Bern. Famine, war, religious unrest, and economic difficulties had forced thousands of Germans out of the upper Rhine Valley after 1708. Many migrated to London and were quickly identified as potential New World colonists. In 1710 a Swiss company planning a settlement in North Carolina turned to these refugees. Baron Christoph von Graffenried, a member and representative of the company, recruited several hundred hardy colonists from the refugees in London. After a difficult journey overland from the James River in Virginia, the Germans arrived at the junction of the Trent and Neuse rivers in early September 1710. They were soon joined by a hundred impoverished Swiss immigrants.

Despite setbacks at the start, von Graffenried's colony, named after the Swiss city of Bern, quickly blossomed. Within a year, the displaced Palatines had built a thriving community. Talk of moving the shifting seat of government from the Albemarle to a permanent site at New Bern began to circulate. This would finally occur, amidst much controversy, when Tryon's Palace was completed in 1770.

But, within two weeks of the settlement's first anniversary, New Bern's situation had altered considerably. On 22 September 1711 the Tuscarora War broke out in North Carolina. The creation of New Bern, where the Indian town of Chattoka had once stood, helped to precipitate a struggle that would become a major turning point in Carolina history for Indians and non-Indians alike.

Despite the activity and enterprise of Carolina's eighteenth-century coastal towns, none would become a Boston or a Philadelphia or a Charleston. In part, geography slowed commercial growth. Beaufort had easy access to the sea but no river links to inland regions. Bath had waterways to the hinterlands but stood fifty difficult miles away from the open ocean. Important as the staples of the young colony were, most lumber and naval stores found their way elsewhere to be fashioned into ships; no great shipbuilding center took root. North Carolina would never be known for her cities. As small farms prevailed in the countryside, small towns persisted on the coast.

Baron Christoph von Graffenried (1661–1743). Thomas P. de Graffenried, *The de Graffenried Family Scrap Book* (Charlottesville, 1958).

Graffenried wrote of his settlement at New Bern: " . . . since there is in the whole province only one poor water mill, the people of means have hand mills, while the poor pound their corn in a hollow piece of oak and sift the cleanest through a basket. This takes much time. Our people on the contrary sought out convenient water brooks and in that way, according to the condition of the water and the strength of the current, made themselves regular stamping mills by which the corn was ground, and the good man-of-the-house had time to do other work." Todd, ed., *Founding of New Bern.*

The Tuscarora War

The tiny Algonquian tribes of the Albemarle were naturally the first to feel the effects of white settlements in North Carolina. As clapboard houses occupied old hunting grounds and cattle destroyed cornfields, the Chowanoc and Weapemeoc Indians gradually abandoned their lands. Some fled south, where they joined with the larger, more unified Tuscarora tribe. Others were bound into the colonial social structure as indentured servants or slaves. By 1700 scarcely five hundred Indians remained in the Albemarle region.

For years the Tuscaroras, an agricultural tribe related to the Iroquois, had inhabited the North Carolina Coastal Plain west of the Algonquians. According to one early eighteenth-century report, the Tuscaroras lived in fifteen different villages scattered throughout the Pamlico and Neuse River drainage basins. By the 1670s the Tuscaroras were aware that the Albemarle settlement was overspilling its bounds and the colonial government was extending its control southward. Immigrants by the hundreds invaded Tuscarora territory.

Soon traders circulated among the Tuscaroras, exchanging rum and other European goods for deerskins, furs, and Indian slaves captured from other tribes. Some Indians became addicted to liquor. Others feared enslavement themselves. Complaints of harsh treatment by traders were common. Before long the colonial population of the Pamlico region had grown enough to warrant the formation of Bath County. By 1700 settlements appeared on the Neuse River. In 1706, while the town of Bath was being incorporated, settlers crossed the Neuse and took up residence on its south shore. The Tuscarora hunting grounds shrank still further. Then in 1710 over four hundred German and Swiss settlers arrived to establish the town of New Bern on the Neuse River. The beleaguered Tuscaroras became desperate. On 22 September 1711 the situation exploded. The Tuscarora War, which would nearly halve the Indian population of eastern North Carolina, had begun.

Although the conditions leading up to the war were manifold, John Lawson put the situation quite plainly in his observation of the previous decade: "They are really better to us than we are to them; they always give us Victuals at their Quarters, and take care we are arm'd against Hunger and Thirst: We do not do so by them (generally speaking) but let them walk by our Doors Hungry, and do not often relieve them." Specifically, the outbreak of hostilities can be narrowed down to three Indian grievances: the practices of white traders; Indian enslavement; and, most importantly, land encroachment. Divi-

(Left) William Bartram's illustration of the Venus's flytrap, the great blue heron, and the American lotus. William's father, John Bartram, called the flytrap "tipitiwitchet." William called it a "sportive" vegetable. Joseph Ewan, ed., *William Bartram: Botanical and Zoological Drawings, 1756–1788* (Philadelphia, 1968).

Bullfrog and Lady's-slipper. Catesby, *Natural History*, vol. 2.

The Cherokee and other tribes explained eclipses as attempts of a great frog in the sky to swallow the sun or moon. When the earth became dark, the people would gather, fire guns, beat drums, and frighten off the frog. Then the sun would shine forth again.

Treating with the Catawba Indians in Rowan and Anson counties in 1754, the commissioners heard King Hagler complain of the whites' selling alcoholic drink to the Indians: "Brothers here is One thing You Yourselves are to Blame very much in, That is You Rot Your grain in Tubs, out of which you take and make Strong Spirits   You sell it to our young men and give it them, many times; they get very Drunk with it   this is the Very Cause that they oftentimes Commit these Crimes that is Offencive to You and us . . . it is very bad for our people, for it Rots their guts and Causes our men to get very sick and many of our people has Lately Died by the Effects of that strong Drink, and I heartily wish You would do something to prevent Your People from Dareing to Sell or give them any of that Strong Drink." Saunders, ed., *Colonial Records*, vol. 5.

The fine for trading unlawfully with the Indians was ten thousand pounds of tobacco, half to go to the apprehender, half to the Lords Proprietors.

sions among white colonists may have further aggravated the already tense situation.

North Carolina colonists realized the potential for profits in the fur trade even in the colony's earliest years. In 1669, only four years after their first meeting in Pasquotank County, the Albemarle County assembly passed "An Act Prohibiting Strangers Trading with the Indians." Likewise the Carolina proprietors stressed the need "to take spetiall care to prohibit all trade and commerce between the Indians and any others that are not freeholders of our Province of Carolina." Although the effort to eliminate competition in the Indian trade was not altogether successful, it certainly allowed Carolina traders to boost the price of their goods. One colonist wrote of "some turbulent Carolinians, who cheated those Indians in trading." Indeed, wrote John Lawson of the deerskin trade, "the Dealers therein have throve as fast as any Men, and the soonest rais'd themselves of any People I have known in *Carolina*."

For the Tuscaroras, the price of European goods was doubly important. In addition to consuming such items themselves, the Tuscaroras had developed a sizable trade as middlemen carrying goods (especially rum) to the Siouan tribes in the Carolina interior. According to Lawson, who wrote in the first decade of the eighteenth century, the Indians of the Piedmont "never knew what it [rum] was, till within very few Years. Now they have it brought them by the *Tuskeruro's* . . . who carry it in Rundlets several hundred Miles." The Tuscaroras also traded mats, wooden bowls, and ladles for skins from inland tribes, "hating that any of these Westward *Indians* should have any Commerce with the *English* which would prove a Hinderance to their Gains."

Among the goods the Tuscaroras exchanged for European wares were Indian slaves. Even before contact with Europeans, the Tuscaroras had kept captives from enemy tribes as slaves. (Though such slaves had little status in the Indian community, they had considerably more freedom than slaves in European society.) Now, however, the Tuscaroras sold their prisoners to European traders, who shipped them to the West Indies or other mainland colonies. John Lawson commented that Indian slaves "learn Handicraft-Trades very well and speedily."

But, just as the Tuscaroras captured and sold other Indians as slaves, so they also became slaves. In 1690 a Virginia colonist shipped "four of the Tuskaroro Indians out of this Country" as slaves. Meanwhile, hundreds of Indians captured in the backcountry had been exported out of the growing port of Charleston, farther south. By 1705 enslavement of Carolina Indians had become so prevalent in Pennsylvania that the colonists feared an uprising. Finally the Pennsylvania Council moved to halt further importation of Indian slaves from Carolina.

Although the Tuscarora grievances over trade practices and enslavement were certainly significant, the Indians' loudest complaints were over land policy. As more and more settlers flocked into the Pamlico region, misunderstandings increased between planters, who claimed perpetual and exclusive ownership of property, and Indian hunters, who expected continued access to the land. According to two Tuscarora Indians John Lawson encountered at the Eno River near present-day Durham, the English settlers "were very wicked People" who "threatened the Indians for Hunting near their Plantations." A settler writing after the Tuscarora War claimed that one of its main causes was colonists who "would not allow them to hunt near their plantations, and under that pretence took away from them their game, arms, and ammunition."

Although large-scale conflict did not erupt until 1711, numerous minor incidents occurred in the years before. The Coree Indians, a tiny Algonquian tribe inhabiting what we now know as Carteret County, rose against local settlers in 1703. In 1704 other coastal Indians raided the home of a colonist named Powell. When Powell threatened to inform a nearby colonial official of the matter, the Indian leader retorted that the official "might kiss his arse." Near this time, a Bath County observer reported that "ye neighbouring towns of ye Tuscororah Indians are of late dissatisfied with ye Inhabitants of this place." By 1707 Pamlico River settlers "expected ye Indians everyday to come and cut their throats."

The settlement of New Bern in 1710 pushed the Indians to the point of desperation. Over four hundred Swiss and German Palatines, led by the Baron Christoph von Graffenried, displaced the Indian town of Chattoka at the junction of the Neuse and Trent rivers. Fearful of further colonial expansion, the Tuscaroras appealed to the Pennsylvania colony for asylum. In 1710, at a meeting with Pennsylvania commissioners and local Shawnee and Conestoga Indian leaders, Tuscarora emissaries proposed to relocate from North Carolina to the Susquehanna region. They sought a "lasting peace" with the Indians and government of Pennsylvania in order to "be secured against those fearful apprehensions they have these several years felt." The Pennsylvania commissioners, however, stipulated that the Tuscaroras present a certificate of good behavior from their North Carolina neighbors before they could "be assured of a favorable reception" in Pennsylvania. This demand effectively denied the Tuscarora request.

Unable to find refuge in Pennsylvania, the Tuscaroras took the offensive. In early September 1711 the Tuscaroras captured Baron von Graffenried, John Lawson, and two Negro slaves as they journeyed up the Neuse River. The Indians took their prisoners to the village of Catechna, about four miles north of present-day Grifton, in Pitt County. At Catechna, John Lawson quarreled heatedly with a

Laws validated the rights of Indians to their lands and the courts upheld these laws, but settlers transgressed. Minutes of the Council for November, 1717: "Upon a Complaint made by John Hoyter King of the Chowan Indyans that Ephraim Blanchard and Aaron Blanchard had settled upon those Indyans Lands without their leave It is Ordered by this Board that the said Blanchards do attend the next Council to Shew Cause for their so doing and that in the mean time they desist from doing anything further on their Said Settlements." Saunders, ed., *Colonial Records*, vol. 2.

Capture of John Lawson. N.C. State Archives.

Coree chief named Cor Tom. Lawson was executed. Von Graffenried was more diplomatic and lived to describe the experience in word and picture. Known for harboring black fugitives, the Tuscaroras spared the slaves.

On 22 September 1711 the Tuscaroras attacked European settlements along the Neuse and Pamlico rivers. According to Baron von Graffenried, who was still a prisoner at the time, the Indians involved were "500 men strong, well armed." At first it appeared that these Indians might repulse the settlers' invasion of their homelands. By the end of the year, 130 English and Germans were dead, and most surviving Pamlico region colonists huddled together in the town of Bath. Bitter political divisions among the settlers blocked any concerted efforts at defense.

Internal divisions split the Tuscarora tribe as well as the colonial government. The northwesternmost Tuscarora villages had not felt the impact of colonial settlement as had their more southerly sisters and brothers. Because of their lucrative connections with Virginia fur traders, these villages hoped to avoid the conflict and immediately negotiated a treaty with Virginia's Governor Alexander Spotswood. Spotswood likewise wanted to protect his colony's interests in the trade. Already embroiled in disputes over the Carolina boundary line,

46

Virginia had little sympathy for her neighbor's plight. When North Carolina appealed to Virginia for assistance, she sent £1,000 and some material for uniforms, but no troops.

North Carolinians next turned to South Carolina for aid. South Carolinians responded favorably—for they sensed lively profits in the making. Defeating the Tuscaroras would mean far more than helping out neighbors. Victory promised fat financial returns in the form of captured Indian slaves. On 27 October 1711 the South Carolina House of Commons resolved to raise troops to fight the Tuscaroras. Colonel John Barnwell, an Indian trader and member of the Assembly later known as "Tuscarora Jack," was appointed commander-in-chief.

The makeup of Barnwell's force reflected the nature of South Carolina's commitment. Of the 528 men who marched north to Tuscarora country, 495 were Yamassee and other South Carolina Indians. Only 33 were white colonists. The pattern is a familiar one: by pitting local tribes against one another, colonists furthered their own ends at minimal cost.

By the time they neared the Neuse River, most of Barnwell's Indian troops had become disillusioned. Wisely, they were "unwilling to proceed into unknown country where they may be hem'd in by a

Christoph von Graffenried, John Lawson, and a Negro slave, prisoners of the Tuscaroras, 1711, as sketched by von Graffenried, "The Graffenried Manuscript C," *German American Annals*, XII n.s. (1914). N.C. State Archives.

Lawson had been dead little more than a decade when William Byrd wrote, "they [the Indians] resented their wrongs a little too severely upon Mr. Lawson, who, under Colour of being Surveyor Gen'l, had encroacht too much upon their Territories, at which they were so enrag'd, that they waylaid him, and cut his Throat from Ear to Ear, but at the same time releas'd the Baron de Graffenried, whom they had Seized for Company, because it appear'd plainly he had done them no Wrong."

numerous Enemy and not know how to extricate themselves." The Yamassees, who like their commander had high hopes for plunder in slaves, were the only group to remain in Barnwell's force.

In late January the expedition reached Narhantes, a Tuscarora stronghold on the Neuse River about twenty miles upstream from New Bern. Prompted by the anxious Yamassees, the South Carolina forces attacked almost immediately. Although the battle lasted less than half an hour, it was not without surprises for Barnwell and his men. Once inside the Tuscarora fort they found that many of the enemy's strongest warriors were women, who "did not yield until most of them were put to the sword." Although they collected numerous scalps and easily destroyed the Tuscarora village, the battle was a disappointing one for Barnwell and his few white companions. "While we were putting the men to the sword," the colonel complained bitterly, "our Indians got all the slaves and plunder, only one girl we got."

After resupplying at Bath, Barnwell and his troops Set out for Catechna, the site of Lawson's execution. There they found an ingenious fort commanding Cotechney Creek. Named "Fort Hancock" for a Tuscarora king, it consisted of "a large Earthen Trench thrown up against the puncheons with 2 teer of port holes; the lower teer they could stop at pleasure with plugs, & large limbs of trees lay confusedly about it to make the approach intricate, and all about much with large reeds & canes to run into people's legs." The South Carolinians learned from prisoners that a runaway Negro slave named Harry had shown the Tuscaroras how to build the fort. According to Barnwell, Harry had been "sold into Virginia for roguery & since fled to the Tuscaruros." One of Barnwell's demands after the first battle at Catechna was for the return of twenty-four runaway Negroes living amongst the Indians.

The site of Fort Barnwell lies just two miles northeast of the present town of that name in Craven County.

At the conclusion of the first battle, the South Carolina forces retreated seven miles downstream, where they constructed Fort Barnwell. From Fort Barnwell the colonel orchestrated a devastating ten-day siege of the Indian fort at Catechna. On 17 April 1712 Fort Hancock finally fell. The Tuscaroras consented to a humiliating surrender. But again Barnwell had very few slaves to show for his effort, "the Indians being more dextrous than us at taking slaves."

The peace was short-lived. Disappointed by the returns of the expedition, Yamassee warriors continued to forage and plunder in Tuscarora country. Settlers likewise continued penetrating Tuscarora homelands. In the summer of 1712 the beleaguered Tuscaroras rose to fight the invaders one more time.

On 8 August South Carolina again came to her neighbor's aid. As before, profit was at the heart of the matter. Desperate North Carolinians eagerly pointed out the "great advantage [that] may be made of Slaves there being hundreds of women and children, many we believe 3 or 4 thousand." Colonel James Moore would lead South Carolina's forces. This time they consisted of 900 Indians and 33 whites.

West of the present town of Snow Hill in Greene County the Tuscaroras' determined struggle to retain their homeland was brought to an end. Here, on 20 March 1713, Moore's forces began their attack on Fort Neoheroka. For three days the Tuscaroras withstood the South Carolina Indian onslaught. Finally Moore's forces set fire to the bastions and to buildings within the Tuscarora stronghold. By mid-morning on 23 March they had routed the last of its Indian defenders.

The Tuscarora War was over. For the Tuscaroras the cost was bitter: a thousand had been captured and enslaved; fourteen hundred were dead. A handful remained in rebellion until February 1715, when a treaty concluded the war. Most of the Tuscarora survivors migrated northward to become the sixth and smallest tribe of the powerful Iroquois League. In 1717 the few who remained in North Carolina received land on the Roanoke River near present-day Quitsna.

Ironically, the war proved as devastating for the Yamassees as for the Tuscaroras they had subdued. In 1715, when the Yamassee War broke out in South Carolina, Colonel Maurice Moore marched southward with a company of North Carolina troops that included Tuscarora warriors anxious for revenge. As the troops passed through the Cape Fear region, they destroyed local Waccamaw and Cape Fear Indians who had allied with the Yamassees. Over ten years later, a visitor to the region would comment, "there is not an Indian to be seen in the Place."

Among the first Europeans to take advantage of the removal of Indians from Cape Fear was Colonel Maurice Moore himself. Moore took up residence in the Cape Fear in 1725 and laid out the Town of Brunswick. The name evoked the German roots of England's Hanoverian monarch, in order to gain his favor. Only four years later, the king would purchase North Carolina from the proprietors, thus making the region a royal colony.

By July 1726 settlers were arriving in Brunswick Town and the first plot of land had been sold. In the months that followed, the Town of Brunswick and the entire Cape Fear settlement grew considerably. A ferry soon carried people and goods across the lower Cape Fear River.

The excavated ruins of the colonial town reveal the remains of Maurice Moore's old home on Front Street next to the ruins of the public house and tailor shop. Roger Moore's home stood nearby on Second Street. A fenced-in plot marks the site of an old garden on Cross Street. Most remarkable is the ruin of St. Philip's Church, where Anglican residents of Brunswick Town worshiped. The brick walls of the church still stand tall; only the windows, roof, and wor-

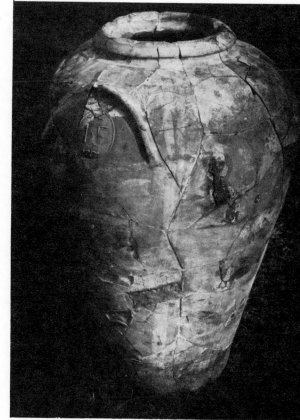

Reconstruction of a storage vessel from Russellborough, home of royal governors Arthur Dobbs and William Tryon, displayed at Brunswick Town. Archeology Branch, Division of Archives and History.

When James Murray was living in Brunswick before settling in Wilmington, he was pleased with the church there: "We are not depriv'd of the advantages of the gospell preach'd for we have the best minister that I have heard in America to preach & read prayers to us every 2d or 3d sunday at least, & in a cold day a good fire in the church to sit by. In these & many other respects this town is preferable to New town [Wilmington], & yet I believe the last will be first in a little time."

49

Ruins of St. Philip's Church, Brunswick Town, Brunswick County.

(Opposite) Brunswick Town foundation stones uncovered by archeologists, Brunswick County.

shipers are missing.

A walk along the Brunswick Town nature trail reveals some of the environment Maurice Moore and other early settlers found at Cape Fear. Spanish moss hangs from the bald cypress trees in Brunswick Pond. The setting is peaceful and pregnant with nature's bounty —the stuff of which Carolina colonists' dreams were made. Only the carnivorous Venus's fly-trap that grows nearby hints that the Cape Fear coast was also a devourer of hopes for the Tuscaroras and other native Americans—if they lingered within the range of land- and slave-hungry invaders from Europe.

Tar kiln, *Harper's New Monthly Magazine*, 18 May 1857. North Carolina Collection.

Pine Forest Plantations

Most of the early settlers in and around Brunswick Town came from South Carolina. By late 1726 leading South Carolina citizens were already complaining of the "Desertions from us to Cape Fear which is occasioned by the rigid usage of the merchants and lawyers." This "rigid usage" was due primarily to changes in the colony's naval-stores trade. As England's navy had expanded during the preceding half century, British officials had become increasingly anxious to obtain vital materials from their own colonies rather than from Baltic rivals. They looked to New England forests for masts and spars and to the southern colonies for the huge quantities of pitch and tar needed to protect the hulls and rigging of England's wartime and commercial fleet. Indeed, sailors applied tar with such regularity (much as modern seamen apply paint) that the men sailing before the mast became known collectively as "tars."

When Parliament began offering bounties on naval stores in 1705, many South Carolina planters made substantial investments in slaves and land. Often, these investments were on credit. The investors planned to pay off their debts with the profits they made on naval stores. But in 1725, after one extension, the Naval Stores Act expired and Parliament ceased paying bounties. A half-century of planting had pushed the pine forests back from the navigable coastal rivers, making rice more profitable than naval stores. Without the bounty, exports of tar and pitch from Charleston dropped from sixty thousand barrels in 1725 to a paltry five thousand barrels in 1728. Caught in the shifts of the lowcountry economy, many planters found they had debts they could not pay in a colony seeking added revenues for defense.

Charleston officials now feared not only the Spanish in St. Augustine but also the increased number of enslaved workers. Two decades earlier, South Carolina's Negro population had surpassed her free white population, and, as the number and percentage of slaves increased, so did the potential for rebellion. By 1720, with the overthrow of the proprietorship and appointment of the first royal governor, blacks outnumbered whites 11,828 to 6,525—or nearly two to one—and a major slave uprising had come close to success.

In 1727 increased taxes reflected the rising cost of keeping the black workers in subjection and preventing incursions by the Catholic Spanish in St. Augustine. For indebted planters dependent on the failing naval-stores industry, these taxes proved impossible to pay. Where summonses had sufficed in the past, in 1727 a new law called

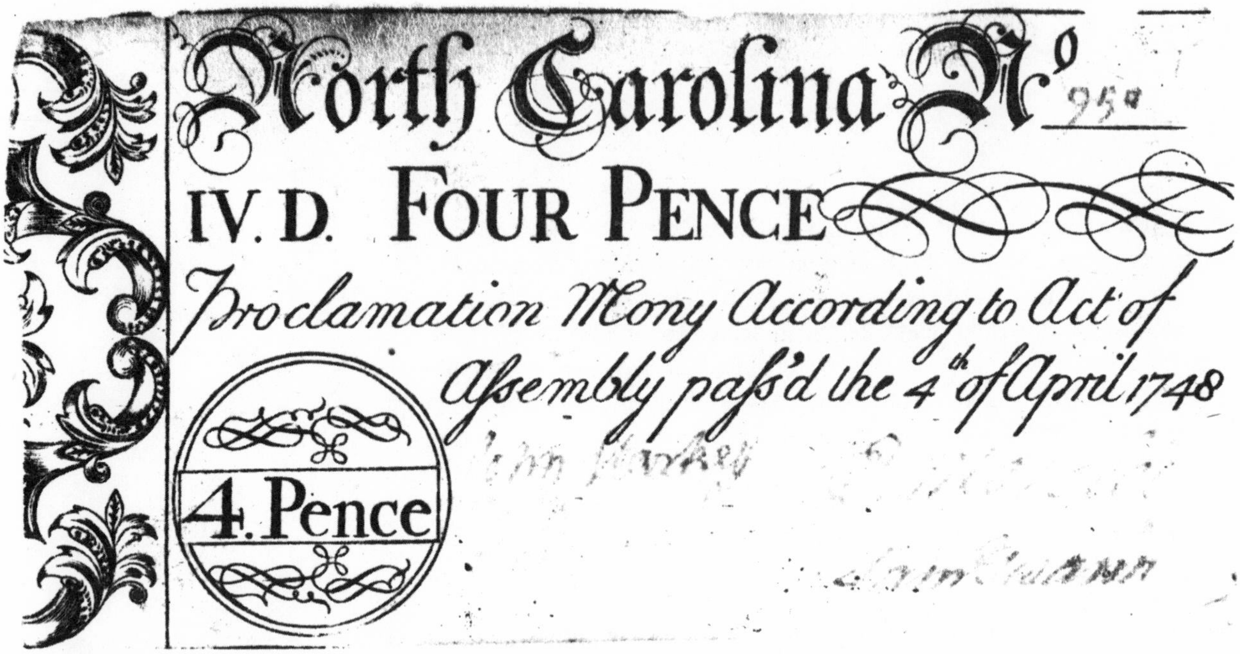

North Carolina N° 95°

IV. D. FOUR PENCE

Proclamation Mony According to Act of
Assembly pass'd the 4th of April 1748

4. Pence

Because Spanish, French, and Portuguese money was far more prevalent in the English colonies than English currency, in 1704 the rate of exchange of foreign coins in English money was set by royal proclamation. In time, laws established rates of exchange as well for commodities, which were widely used in place of money. The term "proclamation money" was applied not only to the rates of exchange but to the foreign coins, the rated commodities, and to paper currency issued with these values.

for the bodily seizure of delinquent debtors. Not surprisingly, many chose to flee. Cape Fear provided asylum to debtors and offered timber-rich land, close to the coast, that could be developed for profit much as coastal South Carolina had been in preceding decades.

In December 1727 an observer described the newly arrived settlers as a "dispersed multitude of People residing up and down Cape Fear." The exact size of this "multitude" is uncertain. It seems likely, however, that many, perhaps most, of the Cape Fear settlers were in some sort of bondage. Both servants and slaves emigrated with their masters. In one attempt to slow the exodus to Cape Fear, the South Carolina Commons House considered, but then rejected, a bill restricting the transportation of indentured servants and slaves across Winyaw Bay and the Santee River. In 1742 the black population of the new settlement was estimated at 2,000 and the white population at 1,000. By 1767 the lower Cape Fear region contained 5,154 blacks and only 2,940 whites. Clearly, these numbers reflect the South Carolina society from which so many of the settlers came.

As in early South Carolina, Cape Fear's chief export was naval stores. Rice exports, which soon surpassed naval-stores exports in the southern colony, were of only secondary importance at Cape Fear. Because of its great stands of long-leaf pine, the Cape Fear region was ideal for naval-stores production. "Most of the Country," wrote Hugh Meredith to Philadelphia printer Benjamin Franklin in 1731, "is well cloathed with tall Pines, excepting the Swamps, Savanahs, and some small strips by the Side of the Rivers." Long-leaf pine yields large amounts of resin, the raw material necessary for naval-stores production.

At the heart of the Cape Fear naval-stores industry was black labor. Skilled slaves at Cape Fear took part in every phase of naval-stores manufacture. They produced tons of tar, pitch, and turpentine annually. The extraction of resin, or crude turpentine, was the first step in naval-stores production. "The Planters," explained North Carolina naturalist John Brickell, "make their Servants or *Negroes* cut large Cavities on each side of the Pitch-Pine Tree (which they term Boxing of the Tree) wherein the Turpentine runs." The workers also peeled bark from sections of the tree so the heat of the sun could draw more turpentine to the surface. The turpentine drained into containers near the bottom of the tree, where, according to Brickell, "the Negroes with Ladles take it out and put it into Barrels." An observer in 1765 claimed "one Negro will tend 3000" boxed trees, "which will rendr about 100 Barls. terpentin." Most turpentine was shipped from Cape Fear in its crude state. On occasion, however, planters had their slaves make oil of turpentine and its by-product, rosin, by distilling crude turpentine with water.

Each tree ran for about three years before dying and falling to the ground. The wood of these downed pines was called "lightwood." Brickell states that during the winter, when slaves could not be employed in the rice fields, planters would "make their *Negroes* gather great quantities of this *Light-Wood*, which they split about the thickeness of a Man's Leg, and two or three Feet in length." Tar manufacture required a large volume of lightwood.

Slaves also built and tended the elaborate kilns in which the lightwood was fired to make tar. They selected a site, usually atop a small rise, and fashioned a concave floor. Then, according to John Brickell, "they take the *Light-wood* which they pile up with the ends of each, placed slanting towards the center of the Kiln." The Negroes covered the lightwood "with Clay Earth or Sods" and carefully set it afire through holes opened in the turf. A pipe that drained tar from the center of the floor led to a collecting barrel outside. The kiln burned continuously for several days and generally produced 160 to 180 barrels of tar. Once this difficult and sometimes dangerous job was completed, the workers could make pitch by burning tar in iron caldrons or pits dug into the ground.

Black laborers stored pitch, like turpentine and tar, in thirty-two gallon barrels, which could be hauled in boats or wagons or rolled down to the docks. Because of the great volume of naval stores exported from Cape Fear, the skilled coopers who made barrels were in high demand. In early North Carolina, blacks and whites alike worked in the cooper's trade, and every plantation had a cooperage to supply casks, barrels, buckets, and hogsheads. James Murray, an early Cape Fear resident, wrote these words of advice to an aspiring

Governor Gabriel Johnston wrote in 1734: "There is more pitch and tarr made in the two Carolinas than in all the other Provinces on the Continent and rather more in this than in South Carolina but their two Commodities (tarr especially) bear so low a price in London (1000 Barrels scarce clearing 20ˢ sterling) that I find the Planters are generally resolved to make no more." Saunders, ed., *Colonial Records*, vol. 5.

"The Rosin is very scarce in these parts, few giving themselves the trouble; but when made, it is done after the following manner, viz. Take Turpentine, as much as you think proper, put it into an Alembick or a Copper Vesica, with four times its weight in fair water, and distil it, which will produce a thin and clear Oil like Water, and at the bottom of the Vessel will remain the Rosin." Brickell, *Natural History of North Carolina*.

James Murray settled in Wilmington, then called Newton, in the 1730s and set himself up as a merchant with a house, adjoining his store, in town as well as a plantation in the country. He described how he wanted the store built: " . . . the whole 22 by 18 on the east end of the house to be lined with boards on the side & plastered on the siding, to be shelved as far as the door from the east end, & counter from side to side with a board to fold down in the middle. I hope the cellar is done under neath, and the sashes according to the dimensions I sent you by Wimble ready to put in the glass."

Murray invited Henry McCulloh to stay in his house in 1741 and described its accommodations: "In my house there is a large Room 22 by 16 feet, the most airy of any in the Country, two tolerable lodging rooms & a Closet up stairs & Garrets above, a Cellar below divided into a Kitchen with an oven and a Store for Liquors, provisions, etc. This makes one half of my house. The other, placed on the east end, is the Store: Cellar below, the Store and Counting House on the first floor, & above it is partition'd off into four rooms, but this end is not plaister'd but only done with rough boards."

Governor Arthur Dobbs wrote to the Earl of Halifax about Wilmington, on 20 November 1754, that the town had seventy families who had built "a good County House or town house, & have raised a large brick church, which is ready for the roof." It was 1770 before the Church was finished. Saunders, ed., *Colonial Records*, vol. 5.

planter: "If you intend to do any business here, a Cooper and a Craft that will carry about 100 barrels will be absolutely necessary."

Such small sailing craft brought the naval stores produced on Cape Fear plantations downriver to Brunswick Town for export. In 1733 the village of Newton, later called Wilmington, was established upstream on the opposite bank. The two towns combined formed the port of Brunswick. Like Michael Coutanch at the Palmer-Marsh House in Bath Town, merchants in Wilmington and Brunswick Town exported naval stores and imported English manufactured goods for local sale. Ships carried more tar, pitch, and turpentine from Brunswick than any other port in the colony. In 1768 some 63,265 barrels, or nearly half of North Carolina's naval-stores exports, left the port of Brunswick. Many of these barrels crossed the docks at Brunswick Town. From the top of Fort Anderson, visitors to the Brunswick Town Historic Site today can see the Cape Fear River and the old location of the town's wharves.

Although the naval-stores industry dominated the economy of the lower Cape Fear, a small quantity of rice also passed over the docks at Wilmington and Brunswick Town. In 1768 North Carolina exported only 82 barrels of rice, all from Cape Fear. By comparison, South Carolina exported 132,000 barrels in the same year. Rice cultivation required even more intensive labor than naval-stores manufacture. Only a few of the most wealthy Cape Fear planters owned enough slaves to make rice-growing profitable. (Large slave ships from Africa rarely, if ever, visited the North Carolina colony; the ports were too small and the coastline too treacherous. Like other imports, slaves were expensive and often entered the province overland—frequently from Charleston.) Not surprisingly, the roots of Cape Fear rice cultivation lay in slave labor.

"The best Land for Rice," wrote a South Carolinian in 1761, "is a wet, deep, miry soil; such as is generally to be found in Cypress Swamps; or a black greasy mould with a Clay Foundation." Hugh Meredith traveled a short way up the Northeast Cape Fear River in 1730 or 1731 and found that "Boggy" swamps for rice cultivation abounded in the region. After sloshing across low-lying savannahs, he reported that the "Water was mostly ancle-deep on them." It was on land like this that Maurice Moore's brother Roger settled around 1725. By 1735 Roger Moore had named his plantation "Orton" and a one-and-a-half story brick home had been constructed.

Although the plantation house, now altered considerably, is the only building that has survived for two-and-a-half centuries, many more homes once existed at Orton in the form of slave quarters. When Roger Moore died in 1750, he left an estate including two hundred and fifty slaves to his two sons. In fact, with so large a number of workers, Orton Plantation was more a black village than it was a white homestead. Generations of slaves cultivated rice in the

A cargo manifest for the sloop Betsy and Nancy, Beaufort, N.C., 21 February 1761. Treasurer's and Comptroller's Papers, Ports, Port Beaufort, 1760–61, N.C. State Archives.

field beyond the present Scroll Garden and in the great fields where flowers and shrubs now grow in front of the house. Indeed, it was their labor, in several senses, that created the opulent home of the Moores.

The black Carolinians enslaved at Orton and other Cape Fear rice plantations produced some of the highest quality rice in the North American colonies. One of the reasons rice exports from Cape Fear appear so low may be that planters shipped a great deal of the grain overland to South Carolina for seed. Like slaves in South Carolina, many black workers in the Cape Fear region may have been familiar with rice cultivation from previous experience in Africa. Those who did not bring such skills from Africa could have acquired them in South Carolina before migrating to the northern colony.

Work toward rice cultivation at plantations like Orton began by clearing the heavy natural growth from the proposed rice fields. The

Orton Plantation, off N.C. #133, Brunswick County. Sketch by Day Lowry. N.C. State Archives. The house was built by Roger Moore before 1734, then rebuilt and added to in 1840 and 1910. Gardens created since 1910 where rice fields once lay are open to the public. The private home may be glimpsed from the gardens.

swamps, wrote Hugh Meredith after his expedition, are "generally well cloathed with tall Timber, and Canes underneath; some with Trees only, others all Cane." Removing these obstacles was no small task. Negro laborers "first cut down the Cane, and all the small Underbrush, and gather it in Heaps; then fall the Saplins and great Trees." The slaves burned the branches with the rest of the underbrush, but left the trunks to rot, "the Logs being little minded, because the Rice is chiefly managed with the Hoe."

Indeed, it was by the hoe and hard labor of Negro slaves that rice culture took hold in the Carolinas. Regulated flooding of man-made rice fields to destroy weeds only became common in the second half of the eighteenth century, and machines to help pound and clean the rice were also later innovations. Rice production in colonial Cape Fear—from planting the grain in the spring to polishing it in the fall—depended entirely upon hand labor. Many of the techniques used in the rice fields of colonial Carolina bore considerable resemblance to those used by African rice planters on the Windward Coast. African patterns are discernible throughout the stages of sowing, cultivating, and harvesting. For example, workers experienced at growing rice in western Africa continued to use the same kind of large wooden mortar and pestle when obliged to clean rice in Carolina. Once the husks had been pounded loose, they were separated from the grains by tossing the rice in large, flat, African-style winnowing baskets, woven from palmetto leaves. The wind carried away the loosened stems and husks. The workers then returned the rice to the mortar and pestle and polished the grains with the pestle's broad, blunt end. Each slave usually produced 200 to 250 pounds (about two acres' yield) of polished rice grains for market.

The prospects for exploiting Cape Fear's bountiful resources had been sensed by early European visitors long before Maurice Moore and his brothers arrived in the region. In 1663 William Hilton had described a land "innumerable of Pines, tall and good," and in 1666 a promoter of the Charles Town settlement lauded "The Meadows," which were "very proper for Rice." Neither of these crops depends on a slave labor force. But experience in South Carolina had taught profit-hungry planters that African workers enslaved for life were the cheapest form of plantation labor. At places like Orton, Cape Fear planters prospered. Just before the American Revolution, one observer noted the extraordinary affluence of whites in the coastal sections of what we know as Brunswick County. Ignoring the harsh circumstances of the region's black majority, or perhaps not even counting them as "people," he wrote that there were "fewer of the lower class of country people than [in] any part of the whole province." Though remarkably invisible to white travelers and generations of historians, the Afro-American colonists of colonial Cape Fear did fully as much as the dominant English minority to shape the region's early economic and cultural development.

A visitor to the Cape Fear recorded in 1734 that Roger Moore, "hearing we were come, was so kind as to send fresh horses for us to come up to his house, which we did, and were kindly received by him; he being the chief gentleman in all Cape Fear. His house is built of brick, and exceedingly pleasantly situated about two miles from the town [Brunswick], and about half a mile from the river; though there is a creek comes close up to the door, between two beautiful meadows about three miles in length. He has a prospect of the town of Brunswick, and of another beautiful brick house, a building about half a mile from him, belonging to Eleazar Allen, Esq." Sprunt, *Chronicles of the Cape Fear River*.

Brickell described the blacks in North Carolina: "There are several Blacks born here that can Read and Write, others that are bred to Trades, and prove good Artists in many of them. Others are bred to no Trades, but are very industrious and laborious in improving their Plantations, planting abundance of Corn, Rice and Tobacco, and making vast quantities of Turpentine, Tar, and Pitch being better able to undergo fatiques in the extremity of the hot Weather than any Europeans."

Spanish moss on a live oak. This kind of
lush vegetation greeted settlers in the
lower Cape Fear.

Long Journey of the Highland Scots

In the half-century after the Tuscarora War, as Africans and Englishmen began clearing out plantations around Cape Fear, the population of colonial North Carolina became dramatically larger and more diversified. When Maurice Moore established the town of Brunswick, North Carolina was England's most thinly populated mainland colony. By the time of the American Revolution, only Virginia, Massachusetts, and Pennsylvania supported more inhabitants than North Carolina. The colony's population climbed from fewer than 35,000 in 1730 to well over 200,000 by 1775.

Beginning in the 1730s a relentless flow of immigrants poured into North Carolina. Newcomers of Welsh descent settled along the Northeast Cape Fear River in the early 1730s. Starting in 1732, Highland Scots moved into the Cape Fear backcountry. Later on, Scotch-Irish and German immigrants from Pennsylvania, Maryland, and Virginia would travel down the Great Wagon Road to the North Carolina Piedmont.

All these European immigrants came to North Carolina seeking better conditions than they had left behind. Some came for religious reasons, having heard that the Anglican church was weak in the colony. Others came for political reasons. Most frequently, however, the settlers hoped to acquire land, inevitably a scarce and expensive resource in their homelands. Smallpox and wars had considerably diminished the Indian population of the Carolina Piedmont. The remnants of the small interior Siouan tribes had joined the Catawba Indians at such sites as Nauvasa on the Catawba River, in modern Iredell County, and Sugaree, south of present-day Charlotte. Only the Cherokees far to the west presented a significant obstacle to white expansion. Because it took the newcomers some years to reach the Cherokee country, hostilities did not break out until the 1750s. In the meantime, the situation was as Governor Burrington put it in 1733: "Land is not wanting for men in Carolina, but men for land."

Around 1730 a group of Welsh colonists from Pennsylvania arrived at Cape Fear to take up some of this abundant land. They followed the Northeast Cape Fear River northward and settled on what came to be called the "Welsh Tract" in present-day Pender County.

Interest in the Cape Fear region was evidently quite strong among Welsh Pennsylvanians. "The new Settlement going forward at Cape Fear," Philadelphian Benjamin Franklin explained in 1731, has "for these *3* or *4* years past, been the Subject of much Discourse,

The general area of the Welsh tract is thought to have been about eight and a half miles north of Burgaw, Pender County.

Gray fox squirrel. Catesby, *Natural History*, vol. 2. "They are injurious to the Planters of Virginia and Carolina by destroying their corn and pulse."

especially among Country People." According to Franklin, "great Numbers" of Pennsylvanians visited the Cape Fear region annually, "that they may be capable of judging whether it will be an advantagious Exchange if they should remove and settle there." None of these travelers, Franklin complained, had "at their Return published their Observations for the Information of others." Hence he took it upon himself to print the account of his former partner, Hugh Meredith, a young Welsh Pennsylvanian, "fond of reading but addicted to drinking," who had recently traveled to the Welsh Tract.

Meredith described a land of "small Ascents and Descents, with fine Runs of Water in the Vallies, passing among Limestone Rocks." Pines abounded in the country's lower reaches, while "good Oak and Hickery" covered the land farther upstream. At one point, Meredith passed through "as fine a Wood to walk in as could be wished, of all the Sorts that are in *Pennsylvania*." Farther on he encountered "the finest Crop of Indian Corn I ever have seen; the Stalks of which measured 18 Foot long."

Despite the publication of Meredith's account in the *Pennsyl-*

vania Gazette, Welsh migration from Pennsylvania was actually quite limited. Before long, numerous families of other descents had settled on the tract. By the time Pastor Hugh McAden visited Cape Fear in 1756, the region's ethnic makeup had broadened considerably. McAden even preached to a large group of Irish who were "very desirous of joining the Welch Tract."

Not long after the Welsh Pennsylvanians began moving to North Carolina, a group of immigrants from a much more distant land reached the colony's shores. By 1732 the first of many Highland Scots had arrived at Cape Fear. James Innes, a Highlander from the northeastern county of Caithness, received a 320-acre grant of Bladen County land in January 1732. Just over a year later, Innes acquired an additional 640 acres, and Hugh Campbell and William Forbes received 640 acres apiece. Campbell and Innes secured even more land later, as they paid for the transportation of additional settlers from the Highlands. As many as seventy Scots may have settled with these men. In the years that followed, until the outbreak of the American Revolution, thousands of Highland Scots migrated to North Carolina.

These immigrants, who made a distinctive mark on North Carolina's culture, were a small part of a larger exodus prompted by drastic economic and political changes in the Scottish Highlands. After the Jacobite uprisings of 1715 and 1745, in which several Highland clans attempted to return the Stuart line to the English throne, the crown imposed harsh punishments on all the Highland Scots. Some of these measures were designed to undermine the clan system and the power

On 26 June 1754 Hector Macalister wrote the following from Scotland to his brother Alexander, newly settled in the Cape Fear area: "The Owners of the Argyle Snow [a square-rigged ship] of Campbelltown [Kintyre, Scotland] have promised to have that Vessell in readyness for me any time twixt the Month of March & July next & on that I have fixed since I coud do no better. . . . Mr. Neill McLeod whome the Coloney wanted over to be their Minister, was to goe with me, & as he is a very popular man amongst the Commonality, woud encourage numbers to leave this Country . . . he is a good preacher and full master of the highland tongue, & am sure woud please all partys. You'll likewise advise me . . . what goods from this place will answer your market best, as all the passengers will bring some with them." Alexander McAllister Papers, Southern Historical Collection.

Hugh McAden, a Presbyterian minister, preached in January 1756 "to a number of Highlanders" at Hector McNeill's; "some of them scarcely knew one word that I said—the poorest singers I ever heard in all my life." Saunders, ed., *Colonial Records*, vol. 5.

John White drawing. N.C. State Archives.

Settlers had to contend with wild and unfamiliar animals. "Bevers are very numerous in *Carolina*, there being abundance of their Dams in all Parts of the Country, where I have travel'd. They are the most industrious and greatest Artificers . . . of any four-footed Creatures in the World. Their Food is chiefly the Barks of Trees and Shrubs, viz: Sassafras, Ash, Sweet-Gum and several others. If you take them young, they become very tame and domestick, but are very mischievous in spoiling Orchards, by breaking the Trees, and blocking up your Doors in the Night, with the Sticks and Wood they bring thither." Lawson, *A New Voyage to Carolina.*

of the clan chiefs. The Highland Dress Act banned the wearing of distinctive clan attire. Military service to the clan chief—the traditional method of "paying rent" for farmland—was forbidden. As real rents inevitably climbed, many tenants were forced from their land and clan chiefs lost some of their authority.

In addition, as agricultural methods improved in the Scottish Highlands, farmers ceased choosing farmland by lottery each spring, and instead worked the same plots each year. Cooperation declined as farmers strove to improve and expand their own plots. The introduction of the metal plow drastically decreased the amount of labor needed for farming. Lowlanders soon introduced sheep to the Highlands. "Enclosures" followed, as farmland was fenced in to create pastures for grazing. Lastly, the spread of the new inoculation process to curb death from smallpox combined with other factors to bring about considerable population growth. There was not only less available land, but more people as well.

Before reaching the more plentiful land of Carolina, the Highland Scots, like other transatlantic migrants, had to endure a long and grueling ocean voyage. Often it was this voyage, not the actual settlement of land in Carolina, that proved most difficult for the immigrants. The journey could last from one to two months. Living quarters on shipboard were usually below deck—damp, dark, and airless. At times disease rampaged among the tightly housed Highlanders. Ship captains often violated their contracts and failed to supply the food they had promised. Mortality rates on these voyages were notoriously high. In *The Highland Scots of North Carolina*, Duane Meyer describes the experience of a shipful of Scots in 1774, journeying to North Carolina and the West Indies aboard the *Jamaica Packet*:

> The settlers had been forced to leave the Highlands because of high rents. Crowded in a small compartment below deck, the passengers were once confined for a nine-day period during a sea storm. The compartment was ventilated only by the cracks in the deck above them, which also allowed the sea to run in when the deck was awash. According to contract, they were to have received each week one pound of meat, two pounds of oatmeal, a small quantity of biscuit, and some water. The provisions actually supplied them consisted of spoiled pork, moldy biscuit, oatmeal, and brackish water. The passengers were fortunate to have potatoes, which were eaten raw and used to supplement their diet. For this fare and these accommodations, they were charged double the usual transportation fees because it was late October and all the other ships had gone when they arrived. Having only enough money for the regular charges, they were forced to sell themselves to the ship owner as indentured servants in order to pay for their transportation. Poorly

nourished as they were and dreading the prospect of indentured servitude, the unfortunate passengers were set upon by the crew at the crossing of the Tropic of Cancer. On threat of dragging the emigrants behind the ship with a rope, the sailors attempted to extort the little property they still possessed.

Scots bound for North Carolina almost invariably landed at Cape Fear. Unlike other North Carolina rivers, the lower Cape Fear was navigable by seagoing vessels for over twenty miles upstream. Although they disembarked at both Brunswick Town and Wilmington, the arriving Highlanders preferred the latter site because it placed them closer to the backcountry. After landing, they transferred their belongings to longboats, canoes, or other small craft and made their way up the Cape Fear River. Ninety miles upstream, at the site of present-day Fayetteville, they debarked for the last time.

For part of the eighteenth century, the city we now know as Fayetteville actually consisted of two different towns. Cross Creek, founded about 1760, quickly became the commercial hub of the Cape Fear backcountry. The town's name derived from its location at the junction of two creeks that, according to folk tradition, crossed without mixing currents. In 1762 the colonial Assembly passed a bill establishing the town of Campbellton nearby. The Assembly intended Campbellton to become the trading center of the upper Cape Fear, but because of the town's inferior location and late start, it never caught up with neighboring Cross Creek. Campbellton's deficiencies were not lost on residents of the surrounding county, a group of whom wrote: " . . . the situation of Cross Creek is High, dry, and healthy, and accomodated with Excellent Water, & that of Campbellton, as laid out by act of Assembly, is mostly in a low, swampy situation, & the road from Cross Creek thereto is through a level clay ground, which from the constant intercourse of Wagons, is often rendered almost impassable for foot persons and extremely disagreeable to horse men." In order to allay these problems, Campbellton and Cross Creek merged in 1778 and in 1783 assumed the name of Fayetteville to honor General Lafayette, the French aristocrat who served in the patriot cause during the American Revolution.

Although those Highlanders who were merchants or artisans settled in the town of Cross Creek, most of the immigrants took up farmland in the surrounding countryside. Some newcomers, such as those aboard the *Jamaica Packet*, arrived as indentured servants and farmed the land of others. But those who could pay their transportation to the colony usually bought their own land. Fields had to be cleared and homes built before the first seeds could be sown. Like the Indians described by John Lawson years before, farmers in the Carolina backcountry cleared their land by girdling, not cutting, the trees. The stumps and trees left in the fields made plowing difficult.

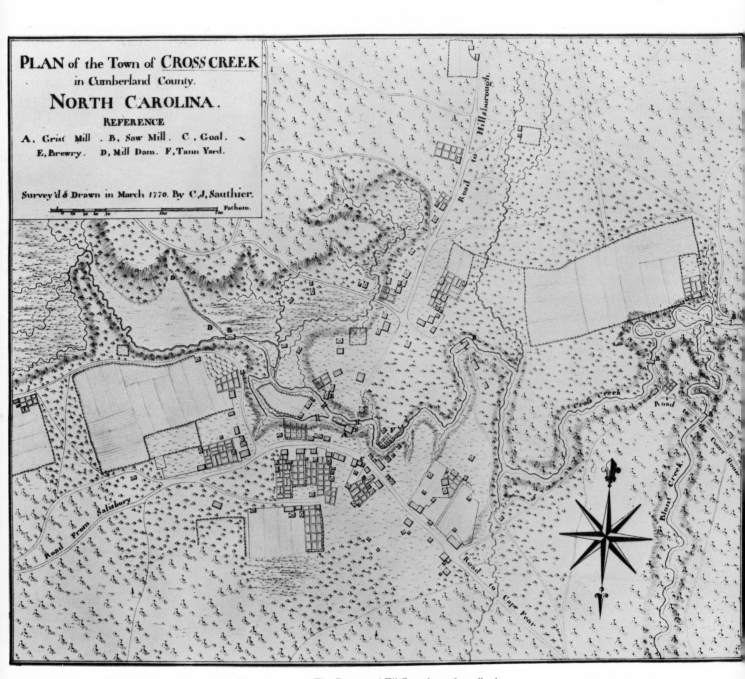

PLAN of the Town of CROSS CREEK in Cumberland County. NORTH CAROLINA.

REFERENCE
A. Grist Mill . B, Saw Mill . C, Goal .
E, Brewry . D, Mill Dam . F, Tann Yard.

Survey'd & Drawn in March 1770. By C. J, Sauthier.

C. J. Sautier's "Plan of the Town of Cross Creek," 1770. N.C. State Archives.

The Reverend Eli Caruthers described a typical backcountry house: "His house, like most others then in the country, was a small log house, with a potato hole under the floor and directly in front of the fire-place, the access to which was by raising two or three planks which extended only across the first two sleepers and were left unfastened for the purpose."

Most settlers relied on hoes in the early years. The crops Highland Scots produced along the upper Cape Fear were similar to those grown in the Albemarle. Corn predominated among foodstuffs. Legumes, wheat, flax, oats, potatoes, and tobacco could also be found in backcountry fields.

In the Highlands of Scotland, where wood was scarce, homes were built of stone and sod; wooden furniture was rare. Highland Scots burned peat in a central pit for heat, and let the smoke rise through a hole in the roof. In North Carolina, however, wood was so abundant that settlers from the British Isles began referring to it as "lumber," their term for anything useless, cumbersome, and in the way. Highlanders on the upper Cape Fear built log homes chinked with clay. They constructed lofts, floors, and porches of wood. Hardwood logs were burned in fireplaces for warmth in winter.

By the time of the American Revolution, as many as ten thousand Highland Scots may have settled along the Cape Fear and its tributaries. There they found an abundance of land and resources unheard of in their native Scotland. But it was not just newcomers from Wales and the Scottish Highlands who swelled North Carolina's population in the mid-eighteenth century. While these settlers pushed back the Cape Fear frontier, Scotch-Irish and German immigrants poured into North Carolina by another route: the Great Wagon Road.

Byrd observed backcountry ingenuity in the houses he saw west of Edenton: "Most of the Houses of this Part of the Country are Log-houses, covered with Pine or Cypress Shingles, 3 feet long, and one broad. They are hung upon Laths with Peggs, and their doors too turn upon Wooden Hinges, and have wooden Locks to Secure them, so that the Building is finisht without Nails or other Iron-Work. They also set up their Pales [fences] without any Nails at all, and indeed more Securely than those that are nail'd."

N.C. State Archives.

The Great Wagon Road

After 1735, as the supply of land grew short in the northern colonies, numerous farmers from Pennsylvania, Maryland, and Virginia began packing their possessions and making the long journey to the North Carolina Piedmont. At first the migrants were predominantly Scotch-Irish. Then, in the mid-1700s, Pennsylvania Germans joined their neighbors on a tedious trek. As newcomers flocked southward, the population of the North Carolina backcountry grew at an unprecedented rate. The path to Carolina came to be called the Great Wagon Road. "The country," wrote colonist Nathaniel Rice in 1752, "is in a flourishing condition, the western parts settling very fast."

The diverse backgrounds of the immigrants shaped the North Carolina backcountry into a patchwork of religious and cultural enclaves. Many newcomers from Pennsylvania were Quakers. Newly arrived German families were predominantly Lutheran, with the notable exception of the Moravians. Immigrants of Scotch heritage were almost invariably Presbyterian. In addition, the Great Awakening, a tremendous religious revival that swept the English colonies in the mid-eighteenth century, resulted in the founding of several Baptist churches in the Carolina backcountry.

The Presbyterian Scotch-Irish were among the first Europeans to settle in the rolling hills of the North Carolina Piedmont. Surprisingly little is known of these early immigrants. Some of them were second-generation Americans, whose parents had settled on the rich farmlands of Pennsylvania. Others were newly arrived migrants from Ulster, who landed in Philadelphia and immediately journeyed south. The Scotch-Irish appear to have taken up land throughout the North Carolina Piedmont, but, because they left so little evidence behind, the number that came to the colony is uncertain.

The Scotch-Irish were actually Lowland Scots who had moved to the region around Ulster, Ireland, in the seventeenth and early eighteenth centuries. The English crown encouraged Scotch migration to Ulster in hopes that the Scots would "civilize" the Irish. Whether or not the Scots managed to alter the Irish, they certainly managed to advance themselves. By 1700 the flourishing Irish woolen industry had become a threat to the industry in England. The crown soon passed the Woolen Act to protect the textile industry at home. Before long, economic depression set in around Ulster. Rents went up and crops failed. Disease destroyed numerous sheep. By 1718 the first group of Scotch-Irish immigrants had set out for North America, and further migrations followed.

Conestoga wagon. Bogart, *Economic History*. These wagons were developed in Conestoga, Pennsylvania, to transport settlers and their possessions over the rough trails to their new homes in the wilderness. The slightly upcurved ends were to prevent the shifting of their loads going up and down hills, and the poke-bonnetlike canvas hood protected the passengers from dust, sun, and rain on their long journeys.

Joel McLendon House (ca. 1760), S.R. #1210 seven miles west of Carthage, Moore County. The log structure, whose batten door and strap hinges still remain, was built by a Scots-Irishman who also had a mill on the nearby creek.

At the time of Brickell's sojourn in North Carolina, the 1730s, water mills were still uncommon. "The Proprietors of these Mills take most commonly every other Barrel as Toll, for grinding; but the Laws of the Country allow only every sixth."

Most of the early Scotch-Irish arrivals in America landed at Philadelphia and set up farms in Pennsylvania and Maryland. As these lands filled, some had to take up land in Virginia. In addition, the Scotch-Irish soon encountered competition from German immigrants (who, coming from "Deutschland," were incorrectly labeled as "Pennsylvania Dutch"). Indeed, wrote one English observer, the Scotch-Irish, "not succeeding so well in Pennsylvania as the more frugal and industrious Germans, sell their lands in that province to the latter, and take up new ground in the remote counties in Virginia, Maryland, and North Carolina." Many of the Scotch-Irish who moved to North Carolina were actually the younger children of immigrants who had settled land in Pennsylvania in earlier years. By the 1730s there was simply not enough land to go around; by 1735 the Scotch-Irish had begun entering North Carolina in significant numbers. They would continue to do so until the American Revolution.

The movement of Scotch-Irish and, eventually, of German immigrants southward can be measured by the progress of the Great Wagon Road. Starting at the Schuylkill River in Philadelphia, the road would one day stretch all the way to the Savannah River at Augusta, Georgia—a distance of over 735 miles. In the 1720s, however, the road extended only to the Susquehanna River in Lancaster County, Pennsylvania. Before long it had crossed the Susquehanna, passed through the towns of York and Gettysburg, and entered the Maryland colony. From there the road took a steady course southwest, into the great Shenandoah Valley. By mid-century, the Virginia towns of Martinsburg, Winchester, and Staunton marked the road's route through the valley. Near present-day Roanoke the Great Road turned eastward and followed the Staunton River through the Blue Ridge. It then turned southward once more and entered North Carolina. By 1760 the road had passed through the Moravian settlement in Forsyth County and extended as far as the town of Salisbury, in Rowan County. From there it continued its southerly course through South Carolina and finally ended at Augusta, Georgia.

Scotch-Irish immigrants like Mary and Francis McNairy from Lancaster County, Pennsylvania, traveled down the Great Wagon Road to make their homes in the Carolina Piedmont. Like the Highland Scots on the upper Cape Fear, most were farmers in search of land. In 1761 the newlywed McNairys bought land on Horsepen Creek in Rowan County (eventually Guilford County) from Hermon Husband, who would later play a major role in the Regulator uprising. By 1762 the McNairys had constructed a two-room log home and started to improve their land, which two decades later would be part of the site of the Battle of Guilford Courthouse. Though the house itself stood for generations beside the revolutionary battlefield, it has since been moved to the yard of the Greensboro Historical Museum, where it is now open to visitors. The McNairys expanded their home to its present size as the family prospered over time. "The inhabitants here and about Guilford Courthouse," wrote an observer years after the arrival of the McNairys, "are chiefly Irish, being very courteous, humane and affable to strangers, as likewise are the inhabitants of the counties of Mecklenburg and Roan." Many Scotch-Irish settlers like the McNairys would later take part in the Regulator rebellion.

During the mid-eighteenth century, Pennsylvania Germans began joining the Scotch-Irish on the long journey down the Great Wagon Road to North Carolina. For several decades after the settlement of New Bern in 1710, few Germans had entered the colony. But by 1748 Germans, too, were being forced southward by the shortage of land in Pennsylvania.

On arriving in North Carolina, the Germans tended to cluster in communities where they shared cultural traits such as language and religion with other Germans. Although they took up land throughout the Piedmont, German immigrants favored the region we know as Rowan, Cabarrus, Davidson, and Davie counties, between the modern-day cities of Winston-Salem and Charlotte. A large number of Germans settled in Alamance, Guilford, and Orange counties as well. Much of the land in these counties belonged to Henry McCulloh. Because of a complex set of arrangements between McCulloh and Earl Granville, settlers who bought land from McCulloh often faced a brutal succession of fees. These included paying McCulloh for the land, paying Granville's agents for recording the sale in the land office, paying once again to record the sale in the county courthouse, and, finally, paying annual quitrents to Granville. Many of these fees, submitted to dishonest officials like Francis Corbin of the Cupola House in Edenton, were illegal and extortionate.

One settler who may have paid such fees was Michael Braun. In 1758 Braun settled in the Rowan County town of Salisbury. Rowan County had been formed only five years before, in 1753, to accommodate the numerous migrants entering northern Anson County. The county court began meeting regularly and soon authorized the construction of a courthouse and prison. On 11 February 1755 the town of Salisbury was officially established. Governor Dobbs visited Salisbury the following summer while touring western North Carolina. After crossing the Yadkin, "a large, beautiful river where is a ferry," Dobbs traveled about six miles to Salisbury. "The town," he wrote, "is but just laid out, the courthouse built and seven or eight log houses erected." Michael Braun, a wheelwright, must have been a valuable addition to the town when he arrived from Pennsylvania three years later.

But Michael Braun did not remain in Salisbury for long. By 1766 he had completed a great stone house that still stands in eastern Rowan County. The two-story home clearly reflects Braun's Penn-

Francis McNairy House (1761), Greensboro Historical Museum, Guilford County. Courtesy Greensboro Historical Museum. When this house was first built, it consisted of only one story and a loft. The Americans wounded in battle at Guilford Courthouse were carried there for treatment.

Michael Braun House (1766), Old Stone House Rd. off U.S. #52, near Granite Quarry, Rowan County. The stone foundation walls of this sturdy and massive house run twelve to fifteen feet into the ground. The family graveyard is across the road, originally an Indian trail to the Yadkin River Trading Ford.

Braun was a wheelwright, planter, and later a printer. He established a German-English print shop at Salisbury in 1794.

sylvania German heritage. Its layout, called the "Quaker Plan," was common in Pennsylvania. The kitchen is a single-story addition off the "great hall." Braun's first wife, Margarita, and later, his second wife, Eleanor, used the kitchen's huge stone fireplace for cooking and baking. A woodstove on the hall side shares the chimney. There can be little doubt that the Braun House is more substantial than most German homes in the Carolina backcountry.

Unique among the German settlements was the Moravian community that grew up on the Wachovia Tract in present-day Forsyth County. The United Brethren, often called the Moravians, originated in fifteenth-century Bohemia, the region we know today as Czechoslovakia. After persecution and near annihilation in the early seventeenth century, the descendants of the Brethren migrated from Bohemia to Saxony, where they settled on the estate of Count Zinzendorf in 1722. There at "Herrenhut" they reorganized and revitalized the three-hundred-year-old faith. But before long they faced persecution once again. This, in combination with an increased interest in missionary work, led the Moravians to acquire a tract of land in the new English colony of Georgia, which was seeking European migrants. From 1735 to 1740 the Brethren built a thriving communal settlement and mission in Savannah. But after five years the outbreak of hostilities between England and Spain forced the pacifist Moravians to move elsewhere. The place they chose was Pennsylvania, where they established the towns of Nazareth and Bethlehem. From these towns the United Brethren did missionary work among both Indians and whites.

Because of their success in the Georgia and Pennsylvania colonies, the Moravians quickly earned a reputation as "sober, quiet, and

Bishop August Spangenberg (1704–92). N.C. State Archives.

72

industrious" colonists. In fact, they were such desirable settlers that in 1749 the English Parliament passed "an ACT for Encouraging the People known by the Name of Unitas Fratrem, or United Brethren, to settle in His Majesties Colonies in America." This led Earl Granville to propose to the Moravians the possibility of a settlement in North Carolina. In 1752 Bishop August Gottlieb Spangenberg toured North Carolina from Edenton to the Blue Ridge in order to choose a site for the proposed community. He selected a 98,985-acre tract in Rowan County, which the church purchased for £500 and named "Wachovia," meaning "peaceful valley."

On 8 October 1753 a company of fifteen men set out for Wachovia from Bethlehem. The party included a shoemaker, a cooper, a nurse, and several farmers, millwrights, and carpenters. These men were charged with the task of preparing the site for settlers arriving the next year. They reached Wachovia on 17 November. On the 19th, the Brethren began work on the town, to be called "Bethabara," or "House of Passage": "The Brn. Nathanael and Jacob Loesch measured off eight acres of land which is to be cleared at once, so that wheat can be sown. Others began to gather the dead wood, and build bonfires. The grindstone was set up, a cooper's bench, and wash-trough made. The Brn. Gottlob, Nathanael, and Grube laid a floor of clapboards in our cabin, for the better protection of our goods."

The Brethren worked all winter long; in the spring they planted potatoes, beans, corn, barley, wheat, oats, millet, tobacco, flax, and cotton. Through the summer they cleared more fields, made churns and corncribs, and built stables, fences, cow pens, and a tannery. Crops were harvested in the fall. Finally in September, "much to our joy," additional settlers from Pennsylvania began to arrive.

This first Moravian settlement is now an archeological park near present-day Winston-Salem. Although a few eighteenth-century buildings have survived intact, the ruins of many structures have been excavated and stabilized. Here visitors can see the foundation of the original Brothers' House, the first building constructed in Bethabara. Just to the west stood the first pottery shop, built in 1755, where Gottfried Aust made utilitarian ware from clay mined at Manakosy Creek. An auxiliary building was constructed in 1756. The tavern, situated well to the north of the other buildings, was erected the same year.

The Moravians also built a great palisade around the settlement in 1756. Reconstructed at the site today, it was intended as protection from the Cherokees after the outbreak of the French and Indian War on the frontier. But the Cherokees never attacked the peace-loving Moravians, probably because the Brethren at Bethabara frequently fed hungry Cherokees and even cared for Cherokee wounded. (Farther west during the same year, Fort Dobbs was constructed on a site just northwest of modern Statesville in Iredell County. The small

Reconstructed stockade at Bethabara, Forsyth County.

Early gravestone at Bethabara. The Moravians proclaim their belief that all are equal in the sight of God by using uniform grave markers without decoration or individuality.

Fort Dobbs State Historic Site, Iredell County. The museum and site commemorate the log structure built in 1755 as a frontier fort for the protection of local families against hostile Indians.

The Indians epitomized the town of Bethabara in their description of it as "The Dutch fort where there are good People and much bread."

The Moravian records tell their side of the story too. They state that at about noon on 4 March 1758 some thirty Cherokee Indians arrived in Bethabara "pretty hungry" and were given dinner at a cost of eight pence each and supper at six pence each. A month later, sixty Indians came. When William Byrd arrived with fifty-four Indians, he paid the bill. Fries, ed., *Records of the Moravians*, vol. 1.

fort, now a state historic site, was built near the foothills of the Blue Ridge to protect Piedmont settlements such as Bethabara from Indian war parties. The fort was attacked only once, and it was dismantled after the war ended in 1763.)

Other structures at Bethabara reveal more local and regional history. The Brethren built a congregation store in 1756. In order to acquire manufactured goods, the Moravians carried thousands of pounds of wheat, butter, and deerskins to Salisbury and then on to Charleston. The tailor shop, also constructed in 1756, housed Governor Tryon when he inspected the Bethabara settlement in 1767. Mrs. Tryon tested the famous Bethabara organ on the same visit. Governor Tryon stayed in the tailor's house again in 1771, after defeating the downtrodden Regulators at the Battle of Alamance.

The United Brethren at Bethabara lived communally, with men and women, single and married, fulfilling separate roles in separate "choirs." Each individual worked for the good of the entire community. Decisions were made in group meetings. The United Brethren chose life-styles, careers, and even marriage partners according to community needs, the advice of the group meeting, and the will of God as revealed in the drawing of lots. They believed in a fundamental equality among all people, perhaps most clearly expressed in the Bethabara graveyard. Here one sees identical rows of inconspicuous flat stones, each marking a seed planted in "God's Acre." With the creation of a larger Moravian settlement at Salem in the 1760s and '70s, another "God's Acre" would be created. For two centuries, deceased members of the Salem congregation have been brought there from the church in town, accompanied by a small brass band, and laid to rest on the hillside. Each departed Moravian is buried not in a family plot, but among the choir members with whom they lived and worked: single men, single women, married men, or married women.

Clearly, the United Brethren at Bethabara were different from other mid-eighteenth-century colonists in the North Carolina Piedmont. They refused to bear arms; they lived communally; they called each other "sister" and "brother." But, despite their differences, the Moravians also had much in common with the settlers around them. Like their Scotch-Irish and German neighbors, and like the Highland Scots in the upper Cape Fear region, the Moravians were first attracted to North Carolina by the availability of vast tracts of land. Also like many of their neighbors, they had migrated from Pennsylvania and did not adhere to the Anglican faith.

Benjamin Franklin estimated as early as 1763 that Pennsylvania had lost 10,000 families, or 40,000 people, to North Carolina. Certainly Maryland and Virginia lost numerous colonists as well. By the time of the American Revolution, the German population of North Carolina numbered anywhere from 8,000 to 15,000 and constituted between 10 and 30 percent of the white backcountry population. Many, perhaps even most, of the remaining white inhabitants of the backcountry were of Scotch-Irish heritage. The Great Wagon Road, more than any other route of entry, had contributed to North Carolina's phenomenal eighteenth-century growth. By 1775 the colony's population would reach 209,550, over six times the population in 1730.

"It is our opinion that Bethabara should be a farming community, not a commercial center, as otherwise there is danger that building and growth there might stand in the way of the new town. . . . Furthermore, it was determined by lot that we are to let our Brethren and Sisters in America know that the Saviour wills that Salem is to be the place in Wachovia for commerce and the professions, and they are to be moved thither from Bethabara." Fries, ed., *Records of the Moravians*, vol. 2.

The Cherokee Indians who visited Bethabara in 1774 heard an organ playing and were certain that children were hidden in the instrument singing. The Moravians opened it for them to prove that there was no deception. Fries, ed., *Records of the Moravians*, vol. 2.

Colonel William Few (1748–1828),
member of the Continental Congress,
the Constitutional Convention, and
signer for the state of Georgia of the
United States Constitution. N.C. State
Archives.

The Rise of a
Backcountry Elite

In the generation between 1750 and the American Revolution, settlers surged into the North Carolina backcountry. "Inhabitants flock in here daily," wrote the colony's governor in 1751. Some of these migrants stopped at the Eno River, near the site of Occaneechi, an Indian village John Lawson had visited half a century before. Here a settlement began that would soon become an economic and political center of the backcountry. Known eventually as Hillsborough, the town became a focal point for the deep-seated Regulator controversy that shook the colony in the decade before the American Revolution.

In 1752 North Carolina authorities established Orange County, reaching south from the Virginia border and embracing all of what are now Alamance, Caswell, Chatham, Durham, and Person counties, as well as part of present Guilford, Randolph, Rockingham, and Wake counties. For newcomers from the north and east, the locale seemed notably isolated at first. When the William Few family moved from Maryland to the banks of the Eno in 1758, eleven-year-old William, Jr., was struck by the region's undeveloped state. "In that country at that time," he wrote in his autobiography many years later,

> there were no schools, no churches or parsons, or doctors,
> or lawyers; no stores, groceries or taverns, nor do I recollect to
> have seen during the first two years any officer, ecclesiastical,
> civil, or military, except a justice of the peace, a constable, and
> two or three itinerant preachers. The justice took cognizance of
> their controversies to a small amount, and performed sacerdotal
> functions of uniting by matrimony. There were no poor laws nor
> paupers. Of the necessaries of life there were great plenty,
> but no luxuries.

In 1767 Governor Tryon wrote to the Earl of Shelburne concerning Hillsborough, "I am of opinion it will be in a course of a few years the most considerable of any inland town in this province." By this time there were already more than thirteen thousand white inhabitants and seven hundred enslaved blacks in Orange County. Almost overnight, to the amazement of coastal merchants and politicians from Williamsburg to Charleston, Orange had become one of the most populous counties in North Carolina. The county seat of Hillsborough became known as the "capital of the backwoods."

As in earlier generations, it was the prospect of land that brought rapid settlement, but most of these newcomers were yeoman farmers who differed somewhat from the dominant class farther east.

The parrot of Carolina and the bald cypress. Catesby, *Natural History*, vol. 1.

"They visit us first, when Mulberries are ripe, which Fruit they love extremely. They peck the Apples to eat the Kernels, so that the Fruit rots and perishes. They are mischievous to Orchards. They are often taken alive, and will become familiar and tame in two days. They have their Nests in hollow Trees, in low, Swampy Ground. They devour the Birch-Buds in April, and lie hidden when the Weather is frosty and hard." Lawson's description of the Carolina parakeet, now extinct. Lawson, *A New Voyage to Carolina*.

They were more often Presbyterians, Baptists, Quakers, or Moravians than Anglicans. They owned fewer slaves and smaller tracts of land. In Orange County in the mid-1760s, three out of every four property holders owned between a hundred and five hundred acres of land. Already a few landowners—one in twenty—controlled more than a thousand acres, but the earliest fortunes were not to be acquired by farmers.

A small network of Hillsborough merchants, lawyers, and county officials prospered first, often at the direct expense of farm families working to clear their land. A decade after its founding, the Eno River town had become the "metropolis of the county, where all the public business was done." According to William Few, the town included "two or three small stores and two or three ordinary taverns." Here newcomers from Virginia, Maryland, and Pennsylvania could obtain crucial supplies and establish credit.

Predictable frontier tensions between debtors and creditors were heightened by the severe shortage of hard currency throughout North Carolina. With little gold or silver circulating in the colony in the early 1760s, backcountry residents were hurt badly. Low prices for their crops meant little cash income. Yet, without cash, they stood to lose everything when time came to pay—in cash—their debts or taxes. Even if a person "has but one horse to plow with, one bed to lie on, or one cow to give a little milk for his children," declared an outraged George Sims in 1765, "they must all go to raise money which is not to be had."

The number of civil cases brought before the Orange County Court climbed from 223 in 1762–63 to 576 in 1764–65. In a petition to Governor William Tryon, Orange County inhabitants claimed the defendants in these cases "were generally ignorant men," who were "in such necessitous Circumstances that their utmost industry could scarce afford a wretched subsistence to their Families, much less enable them to engage in uncertain Law Suits, with the rich and powerful."

When such defendants could not stave off claims or borrow money to meet them, their property was seized by the sheriff, usually at a value well in excess of the money due. Backcountry residents complained not only that "negroes, horses, cattle, hogs, corn, beds, and household furniture" were taken as recompense for debts and taxes, but also that these items were "sold for one tenth of their value" at public auctions—frequently to the friends, family, and cohorts of public officials. In the words of William Few, whose father soon lost most of his property to a Hillsborough merchant, "a fair field was opened for the lawyers."

Among the most enterprising of the lawyers to enter this "fair field" was Francis Nash, the youngest son of a Virginia planter, who became county court clerk in 1763 and was soon an adjutant in the local militia company. In the fall of 1766 Hillsborough was named the permanent seat of the county court. In the preceding eighteen months, Nash's firm had already filed more than twenty suits before the court. His older brother Abner also ventured south to share in the legal and mercantile prospects. Francis Nash established ties with Ralph MacNair, one of the town's newly arrived Scottish merchants, and obtained lots along Margaret Lane near the courthouse.

The opportunities for lawyers and officials in Hillsborough were in large part a result of the increased presence of merchants. William Few recalled that before long "merchants were . . . induced to establish stores that contained a good assortment of European merchandise." William Johnston, for example, arrived from Scotland around 1760 and opened a store with James Thackston across from the courthouse on the southwest corner of Churton and King streets. He was a relation of Gabriel Johnston, the colony's former governor, and a nephew of Samuel Johnston of Edenton, who would later be North Carolina's first elected U.S. senator and one of the early governors of the state.

Thought to be a painting of Governor William Tryon (1729–88). N.C. State Archives.

The Cameron-Nash Law Office (1801), Hillsborough, Orange County, now on Nash's Margaret Lane site, was built by a great-nephew, Duncan Cameron.

Richard Bennehan (1743–1825). Painting by an unknown artist, owned by Mrs. John Labouisse. Courtesy Walter E. Shackelford, photographer.

William Johnston did not hesitate to use his family ties to consolidate his commercial situation. In 1768 he opened a store at Snow Hill, seventeen miles northeast of Hillsborough on the road to Virginia. As a junior partner he engaged young Richard Bennehan, a Virginia native who had been selling merchandise in Petersburg and therefore had good commercial ties to Edenton, Halifax, and a number of Virginia towns as well. Bennehan managed the Snow Hill shop with such adroitness that he became a merchant in his own right. After the Revolution, he became one of the largest landowners in Orange County and founded Stagville Plantation, now a historic site north of Durham.

The handful of aspiring lawyers and prospering merchants in the backcountry consolidated their power through close association with a third, scarcely separable, category of nonfarmers: public officials. Citizens who filled such local positions as sheriff, constable, town commissioner, and overseer of the roads were appointed or nominated by justices of the county court. It was accepted practice to hold more than one public office at a time and to use all such posts for private gain. Governor Tryon himself conceded that "the sheriffs have embezzled more than one-half of the public money ordered to be raised and collected by them."

The very tax structure that these officials enforced was itself extremely regressive. It protected the wealthy and squeezed the less affluent, giving rise to increasing demands that each individual should be allowed to "pay in proportion to the profits arising from his Estate." Residents of Anson and Mecklenburg counties pointed out the inequity of the poll tax, which taxed everyone alike regardless of wealth. "A man that is worth 10,000£ pays no more than a poor back settler that has nothing but the labour of his hands to depend on for his daily support," explained one frustrated citizen. A county tax levied by justices of the peace supplemented the poll tax and added to the tax burden.

The same men who flaunted money acquired by openly embezzling taxes were equally flagrant in charging exorbitant fees. Tyree Harris, the Orange County sheriff between 1766 and 1768, not only collected colonial, county, and parish taxes, but he also received fees for making arrests and obtained commissions for acting as an inspector. He was a preferred customer at the Snow Hill store of Johnston and Bennehan, and when he fled the region before the Revolution he sold Richard Bennehan his home at the confluence of the Flat River and the Eno, supposedly the first brick house in Orange County.

The most notorious of the region's "designing men" was undoubtedly Edmund Fanning. A graduate of Yale who arrived in the backcountry in the early 1760s to practice law, he was what later generations would come to call a "carpetbagger." In less than ten years, according to his enemies, he "amass'd a fortune, of near ten thousand pounds Sterling, and all out of the people." Fanning served as Orange County assemblyman and justice of the Superior Court, while collecting a salary as a colonel in the militia. In addition, he turned a steady profit as the register of deeds. In 1768 local farmers protested that "We the Inhabitants of Orange County pay larger Fees for recording Deeds than any of the adjacent Counties and many other Fees more than the Law allows."

With the fees he collected, Fanning built himself an ample home on Lot 23 in Hillsborough, across from the present-day Colonial Inn. Here he lived in conspicuous splendor, purchasing goods from his associate William Johnston or ordering them from afar. A letter from Fanning to Richard Bennehan, while the latter was still in Petersburg, placed an order for a chair and gold lace from Halifax.

The pretensions of the Yale-educated lawyer soon became more than local farmers could bear. They composed a song heard at weddings and public gatherings in the area that made explicit reference to the flourish of gold lace:

Colonel Edmund Fanning (1737–1818). N.C. State Archives.

> When Fanning first to Orange came
> He looked both pale and wan
> An old patched coat upon his back
> An old mare he rode on.
> Both man and mare warn't worth five pounds
> As I've often been told
> But by his civil robberies
> He's laced his coat with gold.

As for the "civil robberies" of Fanning and his lawyer-merchant-officeholder coterie, the time had come for the populace to "regulate" these grievances publicly.

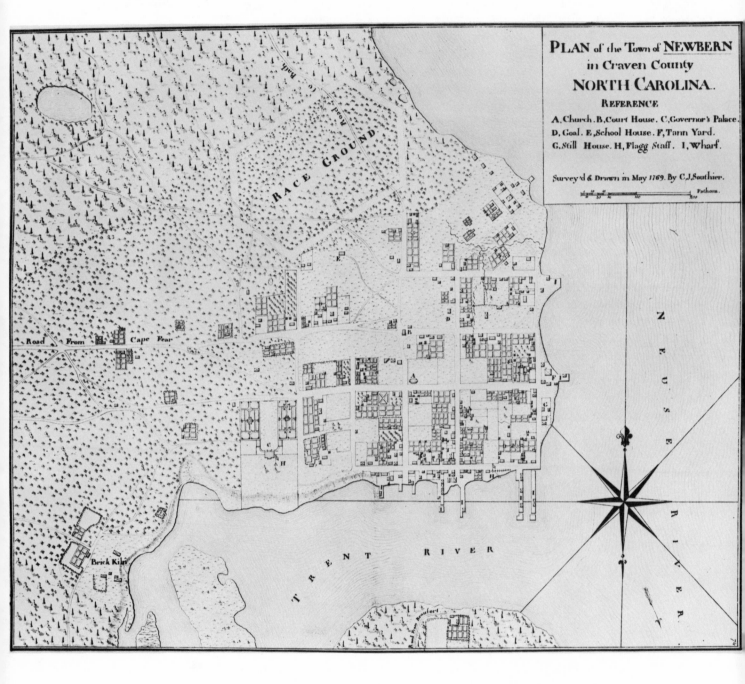

PLAN of the Town of NEWBERN
in Craven County
NORTH CAROLINA.
REFERENCE
A. Church. B, Court House. C, Governor's Palace.
D, Goal. E, School House. F, Tann Yard.
G, Still House. H, Flagg Staff. I, Wharf.

Survey'd & Drawn in May 1769. By C. J. Sauthier.

RACE GROUND

Road From Cape Fear

Brick Kiln

TRENT RIVER

NEUSE RIVER

Rehearsal for Revolution

While Edmund Fanning was building a handsome new home in Hillsborough and trimming his coats with gold lace in the late 1760s, other newcomers to the Carolina backcountry were having trouble making ends meet. Orange County inventories from the period show that the top 10 percent of all residents holding property controlled more than 40 percent of the total wealth, while the lowest 60 percent controlled scarcely one-fifth of the wealth. Enslaved and indentured workers, with no property of their own, made up the bottom portion of backcountry society. At the top, a small elite was rapidly consolidating its wealth.

The resentment of Carolina freeholders at the rise and ostentation of a colonial elite coincided with the Stamp Act crisis that shook the British Empire in America in 1765. Public dissent swept the colonies that year in response to an imperial tax that many saw as the first step toward the subversion of their liberties as Englishmen. For some, the wave of protest promptly came to embrace the abuse of power within North Carolina itself. Citizens in Granville County petitioned the legislature for relief from the corrupt practices of local officials and were met with libel suits by the officials in return. In Orange County, resistance took root in August 1766, when a group of farmers banded together as the Sandy Creek Association and demanded—in the language of the Stamp Tax insurgency—that the North Carolina legislature hear their grievances against local officials who "carry on unjust Oppression." The association's broadside warned that power inevitably corrupts: those "set in Offices and vested with power" will always "oppress if . . . not called upon to give an account of their Stewardship." The Sandy Creek Association called on each neighborhood of Orange County to "meet together and appoint one or more men to attend a general meeting" where it could "be judiciously enquired whether the free men of this Country labor under any abuses of power or not."

The general meeting was set for Maddock's Mill, just west of Hillsborough, prior to the November court session. No liquor would be allowed; propositions would be put in writing and debated freely; "and proper measures used for amendment." Following procedures similar to those being used by New England townsmen at the same time, the farmers planned "in particular to examine into the publick Tax, and inform themselves of Every Particular thereof." The association invited "Representatives, Vestry-men, and other Officers" to the meeting and requested that the officials "give the Members of

(Opposite) C. J. Sautier's "Plan of the Town of New Bern," 1769. N.C. State Archives. Note the race ground.

John Brickell commented on the popularity of one sport: "Horse-Racing they are fond of, for which they have Race-Paths, near each Town, and in many parts of the Country. Those Paths, seldom exceed a Quarter of a Mile in length, and only two Horses start at a time, each Horse has his peculiar Path, which if he quits, and runs into the other, looses the Race."

Stamps issued in accordance with the 1765 Stamp Act, which provoked so much agitation and defiance. N.C. State Archives.

the said Meeting what Information and Satisfaction they can."

Colonel Fanning rejected the association's "jurisdiction" to discuss public matters and banned the attendance of public officials at the general meeting. To join in the assembly with dissidents would give credence to their grievances, he said, charging that the movement, despite its orderliness, appeared too much "like an insurrection." Throughout the fall the situation deteriorated, as Fanning and his associates retaliated against the organized questioning about increased public fees. Hermon Husband, the prominent farmer who helped form the association and remained active throughout the ensuing controversies, recorded bitterly, "The Bombs [Bums] now grew more and more Insulting, taking Unusual Distresses for Levies; taking double, treble, and four Times the Value."

Late in 1766, while most American colonists were celebrating the repeal of the notorious Stamp Act, North Carolina's backcountry farmers were dealt a new provocation. For decades the colonial government had had no fixed seat, but had traveled up and down the seaboard with the governor. A decade earlier, Governor Dobbs had made an effort to stabilize the government and turn a profit by locating the capital upon land that he owned, but authorities in London disallowed the scheme. Already there was growing pressure from the interior to name Hillsborough the seat of government on the basis of obvious population trends. In December 1766 the North Carolina Assembly, dominated by planters and merchants from the east, attempted to "settle" the controversy: it appropriated £5,000 for the construction of a permanent mansion for Governor Tryon at the coastal town of New Bern.

New Bern was an acceptable site for a colonial capital to the powerful planter interests of the northeast and southeast, with their differing origins and economies. But for the underrepresented settlers in the western Piedmont it seemed a real and symbolic offense. The proposed dwelling, which soon came to be called "Tryon's Palace," gave added focus to the discontent of backcountry taxpayers. It linked their grievances against local authorities to the colonial officials on the coast who had appointed them. Moreover, it joined the matter of how public revenues were collected with the question of how public funds were spent.

"We want no such House, nor will we pay for it," wrote William Butler of Orange County, and others in the Piedmont shared his sentiments. Nonetheless in 1767 the Assembly allocated an additional £10,000 for the project and construction began. When the residence was completed three years later despite bitter opposition, Governor Tryon had the temerity to thank "the Country for their Gifts of this very Elegant and Noble Structure. . . . A Palace that is a public Ornament and Credit to the Colony, as well as an Honor to British America."

As early as 1733, some 270 inhabitants of Craven Precinct petitioned the royal governor to establish the capital at New Bern: "We are sensible Edenton is for many reasons a very Inconvenient Place for the Seat of Government and almost as much may be said against settling it on Cape Fear River. Therefore we humbly desire and hope your Excell.^{y} will take proper measures for fixing the seat of Governm.^{t} near the Centre of the Province which we suppose is on the South side of Neuse River." "Petition from the Inhabitants."

Tryon Palace (1767–70), reconstructed according to the original plans of John Hawks, New Bern, Craven County. N.C. State Archives.

Although it burned in 1798, Tryon's Palace was reconstructed during the 1950s and is now an historic site open to the public. Called "truly elegant and noble" by the colonial Assembly in 1770, the palace owes its grand design to the English architect John Hawks, whose eighteenth-century home still stands only two blocks away. Hawks did not withhold care—or taxpayers' money—in creating North Carolina's first permanent capitol: the painting bill alone came to £ 550.

Visitors approach the Palace through massive English gates and proceed down a broad path to the elliptical front courtyard. Separate wings to the right and left contain offices and a huge kitchen, complete with a massive fireplace, a spitjack, and a beehive oven. The central building contains an opulent Council Chamber, with a mantel of sienna marble, as well as elegant living and dining quarters. As if to flaunt the colony's investment and his own ingenuity, the designer focused attention on the Great Stairs Hall, where a beautifully carved stairway ascends around three walls to the second floor without any visible support. Hawks's final bill for the entire enterprise made special mention of "Mahogany for ye Staircase."

Behind the main buildings, impressive eighteenth-century gardens stretch toward the meandering Trent River near its confluence with the broader Neuse. Handsome brick walls create a series of

Holiday preparations in the kitchen of Tryon Palace. Courtesy Tryon Palace Restoration.

garden sanctuaries where modern visitors, like royal officials, can lose themselves in the geometric symmetries so beloved by English gentry of the Georgian era. Discreet marble statues look out over carefully tended flowers and shrubs from both England and America. Closely clipped hedges and dwarf trees grace the Green Garden. Fragrant and savory plants once used for cooking and medicine now prosper again in the Herb Garden.

Early in 1768, as John Hawks began to lay out this elaborate complex in New Bern, "the Rumour of giving the Governor *Fifteen Thousand Pounds*, to build him a House" had reached the backcountry. What Tryon would call "a lasting Monument of the Liberality of this Country" seemed an expensive abomination to settlers in the west. Indeed, wrote a Mecklenburg County resident in a letter to the Boston *Chronicle*, "not one man in twenty of the four most populous Counties will ever see the house when built." The slaveholding planters and established merchants of the eastern counties would keep the seat of colonial government in the east and tax the more numerous backcountry farmers for its creation. Word of this decision, coming on top of harsh existing grievances in the Piedmont, simply confirmed the spreading belief that the governor and members of the

Assembly were men "whose highest Study is the Promotion of their Wealth; and with whom the Interest of the Publick, when it comes in competition with their private Advantages, is suffered to Sink."

As a new wave of dissent swept the backcountry, the organizers began to call themselves "Regulators." The term had been used by farmers in England's Thames River Valley several years earlier and was in current use in South Carolina. There it was applied to the backcountry elite who wished to "regulate" their social inferiors and impose law and order in the wilderness counties. In North Carolina, in contrast, those called Regulators—following a long colonial tradition of organized public opposition to misrule—sought to regulate flagrant abuses of power by their social superiors.

As a Quaker and organizer of the defunct Sandy Creek Association, Hermon Husband found the new group "too hot and rash, and in some things not legal." Conditions in 1768, he wrote later, had given "Rise to what was commonly called the Mob; which in a little Time altered to that of the Regulators." People joined the new association "by Hundreds, and it spread every Way like Fire till it reached Sandy-Creek." Its members refused to pay taxes until "satisfied they are agreeable to Law" and proposed to "pay no Officer any more Fees than the Law allows." By these means they hoped to "bring Things to a true Regulation, according to the true Intent and Meaning hereof in the Judgement of the Majority of Us."

In this volatile atmosphere, Orange County Sheriff Tyree Harris announced that during January and February he would receive taxes on two designated days at five successive places, and anyone who did not pay would be fined two shillings eight pence. "Everyone could see that this Harris' proclamation was quite insulting, as well as an Attempt to make Assess of us," wrote Hermon Husband, whose solid wealth and gift for sharp expression soon made him a strategic supporter of the movement. "This new law was calculated for the Sheriff's Ease," he said. The assessed farmers "were obliged to bring their Burdens to him," so that he and his deputies "might collect the Whole in ten Days sitting on their Greed, at Ease, in five places only."

Some citizens could not or would not meet these requirements, and in April 1768 violence flared. When the sheriff seized "a Mare, Saddle and Bridle" from an indebted farmer and put them up for sale to pay his taxes, a force of sixty or seventy Regulators gathered in Hillsborough. They reclaimed the mare and "fired a few Guns at the Roof of Colonel *Fanning's* House" on King Street. Fanning was in Halifax at the time, but he promptly commanded the arrest of Regulator William Butler and other leaders. Upon his return to Hillsborough, Colonel Fanning had Hermon Husband thrown in jail for "inciting" the band.

The arrests outraged the Regulators. Some seven hundred

armed farmers gathered outside Hillsborough to demand the liberation of Butler and Husband. In fear for their lives, local officials released the men on bail. On the same day, Governor Tryon's personal secretary, Isaac Edwards, who lived in what is now the rear wing of the Nash-Hooper House, read a proclamation from the governor to the assembled Regulators. The governor, he said, "Would Protect and Redress them against any unlawful Extortions, or Oppressions of any Officer or Officers in the County; Provided they would disperse and Go Home." The Regulators deemed the offer a fair one. "No sooner was the Word spoke, but the whole Multitude, as with one Voice, cried out, Agreed. That is all we want; Liberty to Make our grievances known."

In a petition dated 21 May 1768, the Regulators laid out their complaints to the governor. They insisted that the root of their troubles lay in the "unequal chances the poor and weak have in contentions with the rich and powerful." But, despite the promises of his secretary, Tryon was unwilling to deal with the Regulator organization. The Regulators in turn continued to violate the law, refusing to pay taxes and exorbitant legal fees. At last, on 6 July 1768, Governor Tryon himself arrived in Hillsborough to survey the situation. To appease the Regulators he issued a proclamation ordering public officials "not to demand or receive other Fees . . . than what was established by proper authority." The insurgents responded that the proclamation had no effect whatever. Corruption seemed worse than ever.

Tensions increased in September as the trials of Husband, William Butler, and two other Regulators approached. Edmund Fanning and Francis Nash were to appear before court on charges of extortion the same day. To protect the proceedings, Governor Tryon called out the militia. But, because the sympathies of many militiamen lay with the Regulators, he could muster only 1,461 men. On the day of the trial, 3,700 Regulators gathered around Hillsborough while the militia guarded the courthouse. Although the court acquitted Hermon Husband, Butler and the other Regulators received fines and jail sentences. Fanning and Nash, though convicted, were merely fined "a penny each and costs" for their crimes. The Regulators were livid at the outcome of the trials, but in the face of the well-armed militia they chose to disband.

For the next year, Carolina farmers sought redress by legal means. They petitioned the governor, paid their taxes, and worked to elect sympathetic assemblymen. To a limited extent they succeeded; Hermon Husband and several like-minded men were elected to the Assembly in 1769. But even this proved futile. Governor Tryon dissolved the Assembly in November, before the body had time to address the Regulators' complaints.

Late in 1769 the Regulators once again turned to direct action. Riots or other disturbances occurred in Edgecombe, Halifax, Johns-

Powder keg and horn. N.C. State Archives.

Governor Tryon and the Regulators.
North Carolina Collection.

ton, Anson, and Rowan counties. In 1770 the most serious riot of the Regulation broke out in Hillsborough, where numerous Regulators faced trial in the Orange County court. On Monday, 24 September, about 150 Regulators "appeared in Hillsborough, armed with clubs, whips loaded at the ends with lead or iron, and many other offensive weapons, and at once beset the courthouse." A spokesman stated their grievances to Judge Richard Henderson, and after half an hour of discussion angry tempers gave way to violence. The Regulators pummeled a local attorney, and then turned their attention to Colonel Fanning, who had climbed high upon the judge's chair for safety.

Receipt for reward given Thomas Sitgreaves for his capture of Hermon Husband after Husband's expulsion from the General Assembly on 20 December 1770. N.C. State Archives.

According to a newspaper account, "They seized him by the heels, dragged him down the steps, his head striking very violently on every step, carried him to the door, and forcing him out, dragged him on the ground over stones and brickbats, struck him with their whips and clubs, kicked him, and spit and spurned at him." When Fanning took refuge in Johnston & Thackston's store across Churton Street, they pelted the establishment with stones. The next day, the Regulator crowd marched to the colonel's house and, after destroying its contents, "took his wearing cloaths, stuck them on a pole, paraded them in triumph through the streets, and to close the scene, pulled down and laid his house in ruins."

Conditions around Hillsborough, tumultuous through the winter, exploded into warfare in the spring of 1771. In March Superior Court judges protested to Governor Tryon that they could not hold court in the Orange County town. Determined to subdue the Regulators once and for all, Tryon called out the militia. With great difficulty he managed to muster a thousand men and marched them into Hillsborough on 9 May. Two days later, the army proceeded west to Alamance Creek in present-day Alamance County. Five miles away, two thousand Regulators had gathered. Though poorly organized and short on guns and ammunition, the Regulators had twice as many troops as Tryon. Regulator leaders expected the governor to negotiate rather than fight. But Tryon was determined to force the issue. On 16 May the militia moved toward the Regulator camp. Tryon gave the Regulators one hour to surrender. When the skeptical insurgents replied "Fire and be damned!" Tryon ordered the militiamen to attack their

"People in North Carolina differ much respecting Gov.r Tryon's Conduct in the affair of the Regulators; some blame him & some them, & some both of them; but all agree that Col. Fanning was at the Bottom of it: they say that he insisted upon & took larger Fees than the Law allowed; & that when he was in the Back Country he took Money from them for Lands of which he promised to procure Grants for them, but neither did it nor returned the Money; & when they complained to the Gov.r for Redress, he told them he would believe Col. Fanning's Word sooner than their Oath." "Journal of Ebenezer Hazard."

Richard Henderson wrote Governor Tryon on 29 September 1770 of his own brush with the Regulators and of their treatment of Colonel Fanning: " . . . the mob not contented with the cruel abuse they had already given Mr. Fanning in which one of his eyes was almost beaten out, did the next day actually determine to put him immediately to death, but some of them a little more humane than the rest interfered & saved his life. They turned him out in the street and spared his life on no other condition than that of his taking the Road and continuing to run until he should get out of their sight. They soon after to consummate their wicked designs, broke and entered his Mansion House, destroyed every article of furniture and with axes & other instruments laid the Fabrick level with its foundation, broke and entered his Cellar and destroyed the contents, his Papers were carried into the streets by armfulls and destroyed, his wearing apparel shared the same fate; I much fear his Office will be their next object." Saunders, ed., *Colonial Records*, vol. 7.

Alamance Battleground State Historic Site commemorates the Regulators' stand against Tryon.

One of the six hanged was James Few, brother of William Few. Though a Quaker, James proclaimed himself "sent by heaven to release the world of oppression and to begin in Carolina." The Few family moved to Georgia, where William became a leader in the Revolution.

A solitary marker on a grassy knoll south of St. Matthew's Episcopal Church graveyard, Hillsborough, Orange County, indicates the site where the six Regulators were hanged.

fellow North Carolinians. Reluctant to shoot at poorly armed civilians with whom they felt kinship and sympathy, the militia hesitated. The governor stood tall in his stirrups and repeated the command. "Fire!" he shouted, daring them to disobey. "Fire on them or on me!"

The guns of the militia spoke at last, and the Battle of Alamance had begun. The Regulators were wholly unprepared for armed conflict. Many withdrew from the scene when firing started. Fighting ceased in two hours. The Regulators had been soundly defeated.

Several dozen persons died in the encounter. Tryon's militia wounded some two hundred of the local "enemies" and captured fifteen of the supposed leaders. One person was hanged on the spot at Alamance. On 15 May Tryon marched the remaining captives back to Hillsborough with the militia. There the Royal Court found twelve of the fourteen men guilty of treason and sentenced them to be executed. Six finally received pardons. On 19 June the other six were taken in carts to a hillside east of town and hanged publicly before the militia and hundreds of onlookers.

Within five years of the Battle of Alamance, major actors in the War of the Regulation had left the colony. Hermon Husband escaped certain execution by fleeing to Pennsylvania, where two decades later he would lead another uprising of backcountry farmers, the Whiskey Rebellion. Other Regulators dispersed to the north and west, while some of the officials whose high taxes and contempt had goaded farmers to fury also left the region. Tyree Harris moved to Caswell County; Edmund Fanning returned to the North as secretary to William Tryon, who became the last colonial governor of New York. When rebellion swept all the colonies in 1776, many such antagonists of the Regulators joined the Tory side.

Was the Regulator Movement crushed in 1771 a rehearsal for the revolution? Colonists elsewhere were growing more shrill in their attacks on British corruption and more open in their defiance of imperial rule. By 1775 extralegal committees and conventions controlled and regulated life throughout the American colonies: they supervised courts, dictated appointments, commanded militias, and levied taxes. The goals of some of the armed and extralegal committees of the rebellion could not have displeased the Regulators. The revolutionary convention from Mecklenburg not only opposed "everything that leans to aristocracy or power in the hands of the rich . . . exercised to the oppression of the poor," but also favored the exclusion of lawyers, clerks, and sheriffs from the legislature.

Yet, for all the radicalism of its rhetoric, many who joined the independence movement against England wanted no part of a social revolution at home. An authentic civil struggle, modeled on the Regulator campaign against the "rich and powerful"—against the "designing Monsters in iniquity" who through fraud and "threats and menaces" extracted their "Fortunes . . . from others"—held no charm whatsoever for the planters and merchants who assumed the leadership of the patriots in North Carolina. In the end, neither the Regulation nor the Revolution settled the question of whether the public or the privileged would rule. A standoff in the 1770s, that battle was destined to be fought again and again by North Carolinians and Americans for generations to come.

Acknowledgments

The efforts of many persons have gone into this work. The suggestions that resulted from our public appeal for information as well as the knowledge of experts in many areas have enhanced the quality of this book and facilitated its production. Volunteers who led us to privately owned sites and out-of-the-way places have added materially to the gathering and scope of the information in this volume. To all these contributors the staff is sincerely grateful. We especially wish to thank Larry Bennett, Catherine Bishir, Paul Bock, Thomas Burke, Jerry Cotten, Gayle Fripp, Jesse R. Lankford, Jr., Theresa Pennington, Dorothy Sapp, Michael Smith, and George Stevenson, Jr.

The staffs of various institutions have also aided our research: the Manuscript Department of the William R. Perkins Library, Duke University; the North Carolina Collection and the Southern Historical Collection of the Louis R. Wilson Library, University of North Carolina at Chapel Hill; and the Archeology and Historic Preservation, Archives and Records, Historic Sites, Iconographic Records, Planning and Survey, Historical Publications, and Technical Services areas of the Division of Archives and History, North Carolina Department of Cultural Resources. To all of them it is a pleasure to acknowledge our indebtedness and thanks.

(Opposite) Brickell, *Natural History of North Carolina*. N.C. State Archives.

Brickell, *Natural History of North Carolina*. N.C. State Archives.

96

Bibliography

Alvord, Clarence W., and Bidgood, Lee. "The Discoveries of John Lederer." In *The First Explorations of the Trans-Allegheny Region by the Virginians, 1650–1674*. Cleveland, 1912.

Angley, Wilson. "A History of St. Thomas Episcopal Church, Bath, North Carolina." Report, N.C. Division of Archives and History, 1981.

Boyd, William K., ed. *Some Eighteenth Century Tracts concerning North Carolina*. Raleigh, 1927.

Brickell, John. *The Natural History of North Carolina*. Dublin, 1737. Reprint. Raleigh, 1911.

Byrd, William. *William Byrd's Histories of the Dividing Line betwixt Virginia and North Carolina*. Edited by William K. Boyd. Raleigh, 1929.

Caruthers, Eli W. *Interesting Revolutionary Incidents and Sketches of Character*. Philadelphia, 1856.

Clifton, James M. "Golden Grains of White: Rice Planting on the Lower Cape Fear." *North Carolina Historical Review* 50 (1973): 365–93.

Coe, Joffre L. "The Cultural Sequence of the Carolina Piedmont." In *Archeology of the Eastern United States*, edited by James B. Griffin. Chicago, 1952.

———. "The Formative Cultures of the Carolina Piedmont." *Transactions of the American Philosophical Society* 54 (1964).

Corbitt, David Leroy, ed. *Explorations, Descriptions, and Attempted Settlements of Carolina, 1584–1590*. Raleigh, 1953.

Crosby, Alfred W., Jr. *The Columbian Exchange*. Westport, Conn., 1972.

Cross, Jerry L. "Historical Research Report for the Palmer-Marsh House, Bath, North Carolina." Report, Division of Archives and History, 1976.

Crow, Jeffrey J. *The Black Experience in Revolutionary North Carolina*. Raleigh, 1977.

Cruickshank, Helen G., ed. *John and William Bartram's America*. New York, 1957.

Cumming, William P., et al. *The Discovery of North America*. London, 1971.

———. *The Exploration of North America, 1630–1776*. New York, 1974.

Durant, David N. *Ralegh's Lost Colony*. New York, 1981.

Ekirch, Roger A. *"Poor Carolina": Politics and Society in Colonial North Carolina*. Chapel Hill, 1981.

Few, William, Jr. "Autobiography of Col. William Few of Georgia." *The Magazine of American History* 7 (1881): 343–49.

Foote, William Henry. *Sketches of North Carolina, Historical and Biographical*. New York, 1846.

Fries, Adelaide L., jt. ed. *Records of the Moravians in North Carolina*. 11 vols. Raleigh, 1922–69.

Garrow, Patrick H. *The Mattamuskeet Documents: A Study in Social History*. Raleigh, 1975.

Goodwin, Gary C. *Cherokees in Transition: A Study of Changing Culture and Environment Prior to 1775*. Chicago, 1977.

Gray, Lewis Cecil. *History of Agriculture in the Southern United States to 1860*. 2 vols. Gloucester, Mass., 1958.

Hazard, Ebenezer. "The Journal of Ebenezer Hazard in North Carolina, 1777 and 1778." Edited by Hugh B. Johnston. *North Carolina Historical Review* 36 (1959): 358–81.

Hudson, Charles. *The Southeastern Indians*. Knoxville, 1976.

Janson, Charles W. *The Stranger in America, 1793–1806*. London, 1807. Reprint, edited by Carl S. Driver. New York, 1935.

Johnson, Frank Roy. *The Tuscaroras*. 2 vols. Murfreesboro, 1968.

Kay, Marvin L. Michael, and Cary, Lorin Lee. "Class, Mobility, and Conflict in North Carolina on the Eve of the Revolution." In *The Southern Experience in the American Revolution*, edited by Jeffrey J. Crow and Larry E. Tise. Chapel Hill, 1978.

Kay, Marvin L. Michael. "The North Carolina Regulation, 1766–1776: A Class Conflict." In *The American Revolution: Explorations in the History of American Radicalism*, edited by Alfred F. Young. DeKalb, Ill., 1976.

Lawson, John. *A New Voyage to Carolina*. Edited by Hugh T. Lefler. Chapel Hill, 1967.

Lee, E. Lawrence. *Indian Wars in North Carolina, 1663–1763*. Raleigh, 1963.

———. *The Lower Cape Fear in Colonial Days*. Chapel Hill, 1965.

Lee, Robert E. *Blackbeard the Pirate: A Reappraisal of His Life and Times*. Winston-Salem, 1974.

Lefler, Hugh T., and Powell, William S. *Colonial North Carolina: A History*. New York, 1973.

Joel Lane House, "Wakefield," (1760s), Raleigh, Wake County. Lane introduced the bill to form Wake County and sold the commissioners the tract for the county seat. A tavern as well as a home, Lane's house later offered hospitality to the commissioners appointed to choose a state capital. The house now appears in its 1790s form, but it originally had a gable roof and a front porch.

Another early house still standing is Cascine Plantation Old House (ca. 1750), U.S. #401 south of Louisburg, Franklin County. It is still owned by the family that settled the land. The frame house has double-shouldered, Flemish bond chimneys, a shingle roof, and wainscoted interior.

Lewis, T. M. N., and Kneberg, Madeline. "Oconaluftee Indian Village: An Interpretation of a Cherokee Community of 1750." Report, Cherokee Historical Association, Inc., 1954.

"William Logan's Journal of a Journey to Georgia, 1745." *Pennsylvania Magazine of History and Biography* 36 (1912): 1–16, 162–86.

McPherson, Elizabeth G. "Nathaniel Batts, Landholder on Pasquotank River, 1660." *North Carolina Historical Review* 43 (1966): 66–81.

Merrens, Harry Roy. *Colonial North Carolina in the Eighteenth Century: A Study in Historical Geography.* Chapel Hill, 1964.

Meyer, Duane. *The Highland Scots of North Carolina.* Raleigh, 1968.

Milling, Chapman J. *Red Carolinians.* Columbia, S.C., 1940.

Mooney, James. *Myths of the Cherokee.* Washington, D.C.: Government Printing Office, 1900. Reprint. New York, 1970.

Morgan, Edmund S. *American Slavery, American Freedom: The Ordeal of Colonial Virginia.* New York, 1975.

Morison, Samuel Eliot. *The European Discovery of America: The Northern Voyages, A. D. 500–1600.* New York, 1971.

Murray, James. *The Letters of James Murray, Loyalist.* Edited by Nina M. Tiffany and Susan I. Lesley. Boston, 1901.

Nash, Francis. *Hillsboro: Colonial and Revolutionary.* Raleigh, 1903.

Paul, Charles L. "Colonial Beaufort." *North Carolina Historical Review* 42 (1965): 139–52.

———. "Factors in the Economy of Colonial Beaufort." *North Carolina Historical Review* 44 (1967): 111–34.

"A Petition from the Inhabitants of Craven Precinct, N.C." *North Carolina Genealogical Society Journal* 6 (1980): 107–9, as transcribed by Kathleen B. Wyche from microfilm of the British Record Office document, in C.O. 5/308, part 2.

Powell, William S., ed. *Ye Countie of Albemarle in Carolina: A Collection of Documents, 1664–1675.* Raleigh, 1958.

———. *John Pory, 1572–1636: The Life and Letters of a Man of Many Parts.* Chapel Hill, 1977.

———. *The Proprietors of North Carolina.* Raleigh, 1968.

———, et al. *The Regulators in North Carolina: A Documentary History.* Raleigh, 1971.

Quinn, David Beers. *England and the Discovery of America, 1481–1620.* New York, 1974.

———. *New American World: A Documentary History of North America to 1612.* 5 vols. New York, 1979.

Ramsey, Robert W. *Carolina Cradle: Settlement of the Northwest Carolina Frontier, 1747–1762.* Chapel Hill, 1964.

Rankin, Hugh F. *The Pirates of North Carolina.* Raleigh, 1976.

Rights, Douglas L. *The American Indian in North Carolina.* Winston-Salem, 1957.

Salley, Alexander S., Jr., ed. *Narratives of Early Carolina, 1650–1708.* New York, 1967.

Saunders, William L., ed. *The Colonial Records of North Carolina.* 10 vols. Raleigh, 1886–95.

Sprunt, James. *Chronicles of the Cape Fear River.* Raleigh, 1914.

———. *The Story of Orton Plantation.* Wilmington, N.C. 1958.

Todd, Vincent H., ed. *Christoph von Graffenried's Account of the Founding of New Bern.* Raleigh, 1920.

Ward, H. Trawick. "A Review of Archeology in the North Carolina Piedmont: A Study of Change." A paper presented at the North Carolina Prehistory Symposium, Division of Archives and History, Raleigh, 1980.

Whittenburg, James P. "Planters, Merchants, and Lawyers: Social Change and the Origins of the North Carolina Regulation." *William and Mary Quarterly* 34 (1977): 215–38.

Williams, Justin. "English Mercantilism and Carolina Naval Stores." *The Journal of Southern History* 1 (1935): 169–85.

Williams, Samuel Cole, ed. *Adair's History of the American Indians.* Johnson City, Tenn., 1930.

Wood, Peter H. *Black Majority: Negroes in Colonial South Carolina from 1670 through the Stono Rebellion.* New York, 1975.

1 **Yancey County**
Mount Mitchell State Park.

Swain County
Oconaluftee Indian Village, *Cherokee.*

Graham County
Joyce Kilmer Memorial Forest,
    Nantahala National Forest.

2 **Iredell County**
Fort Dobbs State Historic Site.

Rowan County
Michael Braun House, *Old Stone House
    Rd., off U.S. #52 near Granite
    Quarry.*

Forsyth County
Bethabara.

Guilford County
Francis McNairy House, *Greensboro
    Historical Museum.*

Stanly County
Morrow Mountain State Park.

Map of Historic Places

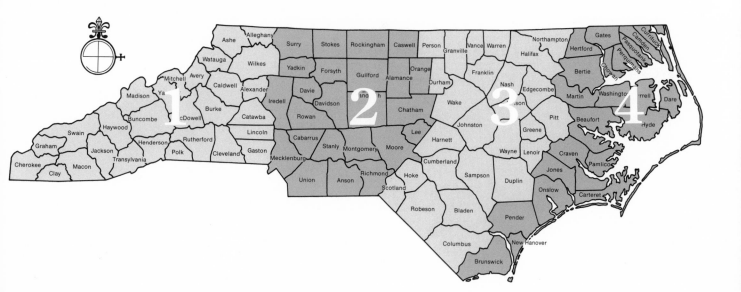

Alamance County
Alamance Battleground State Historic
Site.

Orange County
Cameron-Nash Law Office, *Hills-
borough.*
Regulators' Hanging Site, *Hillsborough.*

Montgomery County
Town Creek Indian Mound State Historic Site.

Moore County
Joel McLendon House, *S.R. #1210
seven miles west of Carthage.*

3 Franklin County
Cascine Plantation Old House,
U.S. #401 south of Louisburg.

Wake County
Joel Lane House, "Wakefield," *Raleigh.*

4 Camden County
Great Dismal Swamp State Park.

Perquimans County
Newbold-White House, *S.R. #1336 off
U.S. #17 bypass west of Hertford.*

Chowan County
County Courthouse, *Edenton.*
Cupola House, *Edenton.*

Beaufort County
Palmer-Marsh House, *Bath.*
Saint Thomas Episcopal Church, *Bath.*

Hyde County
Cape Hatteras National Seashore.

Dare County
Cape Hatteras National Seashore.
Fort Raleigh National Historic Site,
Roanoke Island.

Craven County
Tryon Palace Restoration, *New Bern.*

Carteret County
Joseph Bell House, *Beaufort.*

Brunswick County
Brunswick Town.
Orton Plantation Gardens, *off
N.C. #133.*
Saint Philip's Church Ruins, *Brunswick
Town.*

Index